GAVIN S. JOHNSON

Prisoners of Katrina:

Stranded at Work in New Orleans Parish Prison

A Father & Son Story

EDITED BY

ROBERT SMALLWOOD
and
AMBER J. NARRO

Gavin S. Johnson

Some names have been changed to protect individuals ' privacy.

Contact: Visit http://www.myspace.com/gavin1972

for speaking engagements, media and general inquiries, and group purchases.

Edited by Robert Smallwood and Amber J. Narro

Second Edition.

Cover photo by Lora Johnson

Individual copies of this book may be ordered at **Amazon.com**

Bookstores may purchase from **Ingram, Baker & Taylor.**

ISBN 978-1-4196-6573-8

I would like to gratefully acknowledge Robert Smallwood and Dr. Narro for their assistance.

Fore! U Books

4101 Delaware Ave. #10

Kenner, LA 70065

Printed in the United States of America.

Second Printings of this edition: June 2007

To Lora, whose love and support pulled me through that horrible time; to my family and friends; my mother, Roberta and especially to my father, Liston Johnson and all those who struggled to survive Hurricane Katrina.

Gavin S. Johnson

Prisoners of Katrina:

Stranded at Work in New Orleans Parish Prison

A Father & Son Story

Gavin S. Johnson

http://www.myspace.com/gavin1972

Edited by
Robert Smallwood
and
Amber J. Narro

Gavin S. Johnson

Preface

AUGUST 29, 2005 IS SEARED INTO MY BRAIN and the memory of all New Orleanians. It's a scar as deep as 9-11 was to the rest of the United States. It was the day Hurricane Katrina hit, and I was stranded at my job in Orleans Parish Prison along with my aging father, who had come to ride out The Storm. That week was like nothing we've ever seen in New Orleans, days that will go down in history as ones that changed so many lives in such an agonizing way we may never really know the full extent of the devastation. I saw many events unfold right in front of my eyes; I was trapped downtown before, during, and for nearly a week after the biggest, most destructive and costly natural disaster in U.S. history.

As a psychiatric nurse for the Orleans Parish Criminal Sheriff's Office, I'm an emergency employee. I really didn't have a choice but to stay for the storm.

To make matters worse, my 83 -year-old father didn't even know there was a storm coming. He's very stubborn and independent, making it hard for me to convince him to do much. I was, though, able to convince him to come with me to my job so we could be together and ride out the storm.

We had no idea what was in store for us. This is a story about the love of a son for his elderly father, who suffered through the aftermath of Hurricane Katrina in deplorable conditions. It is a story of families and friends pulling together to help each other survive. It is the story of the unimaginable adversity, danger, drama, uncertainty, and redemption in sweltering heat and trying conditions, and the realization of how much family meant when everything was falling apart.

In light of the ordeal we went through, I wish my dad would have left town and so does he. But the fact he didn't and he stayed with me ended up tightening our bond. I would have done anything for him and did.

With this book, I have told my account of Hurricane Katrina, which is unique in its own right. A Caucasian man surrounded by a disaffected assembly of predominantly African- Americans, I was a witness to and unwilling part of the biggest prison evacuation in the history of the United States.

My colleagues and I worked together in the toughest circumstances imaginable to save ourselves and our dearly beloved city, and show the country and the world we are all one.

Gavin S. Johnson, L.P.N.

Chapter One

ORLEANS PARISH PRISON, IN THE CENTER of New Orleans, is one of the most notorious jails in the United States. It regularly houses over 6,000 prisoners and has a documented history as being one of the roughest, toughest prisons around.

After Katrina hit and the levees broke, electric power went out, and the prison complex was thrust into darkness. Floodwaters swamped restless prisoners in locked cells; some were left in chest-high contaminated waters.

Inmates were trapped with little food or water, and prison guards were ordered to stay at their posts. Some left their posts and many employees, including doctors, nurses and others, had to fend for themselves. It was a hot, hellish week I will never, ever forget.

Thank God my wife, Lora, and our two dogs evacuated early on Sunday morning. My 83-year-old father was a different story. At only 33 myself, I had recently accepted the fact I had to look after him a little more. I never imagined I would have to keep him alive under those unimaginable conditions and circumstances.

Midnight was upon us and it was starting to get pretty quiet. Hurricane Katrina was swirling angrily off the Gulf Coast from

Texas to Florida and would make landfall soon. And it was headed straight for New Orleans.

I could hear the gusting winds outside and by this point, the lights around the city were flickering out. I was on the 10th floor of the House of Detention (HOD) finishing my shift and was able to get a good look outside. It was a light show to say the least.

Transformers were blowing up, shooting sparks. When they exploded, they gave off a purplish-white light and sizzled like colossal sparklers. Amazingly, I could see an occasional car on the road as the rain came down and entire areas of the city started to go dark. Billboard signs blew away and our building started slightly swaying from nature's forces. It was beginning to get daunting. After about an hour of watching the city slide into disaster, I decided I better try to get some rest in preparation for my work the next day.

I took the stairwell downstairs; the lights were flashing and fading all the way down, and then they went completely out, making it as dark as an unlit cave. I waited about half a minute, but the lights didn't come back on. I was between the seventh and eighth floors and could hear some inmates starting to make racket and rattle the bars. Feeling for the handrails, I walked slowly down the stairs into the darkness.

It was eerie.

Thankfully, when I got to the second floor, the back-up generator started and the lights came back on. I decided to lie down on my makeshift bed and get some sleep. The last things I remember hearing were scattered radios blaring bleak messages in a sinister stereo. I could hear the fear in everyone's voices as a somber mood overtook the place. Those around me appeared to realize that it was going to be bad. Real bad. I took one more look at my sleeping father, said a few prayers, and went to sleep.

Tossing and turning all night, I got maybe four or five hours of sleep between unsettling waking moments. That would be the last bit of sleep I would get for a while. A touch of rainy, cloudy daylight crept in through the sliver of a window. My dad started to wake up and sheepishly asked where the showers were.

Laughing to myself, I said, "Showers? Not here, Dad. We could go into the bathroom and use the sink to wet a rag or towel if you want."

Looking agitated, he said, "No, that's all right. I just have to take my pills."

"Help yourself," I said.

The bathrooms still worked at this point, so after he took his pills, we went the break room to get some breakfast .

"What's up Will?" I said to the deputy.

"Nuttin', Gavin. What's up with you?" Will, a young, husky African-American, had worked at the jail probably as long as I had. "Just comin' to see what's for breakfast," I said.

Smiling, he said, "Oh you know, we got those runny scrambled eggs, soupy oatmeal, and some dry-ass jail biscuits!"

"Sounds good. Can I get some for me and my dad?"

"That's your dad? What's up, Pops?"

"Hey, how y'all doin'?" my dad replied.

"Can't complain. You're son's a cool mo fo. Ya heard me, Pops?"

My dad turned to me with a look of *What the hell did he just say?*

A second or two later it must have hit him, because he responded with, "Oh yeah... thanks. He's a good son."

"Let me scoop y'all up some of this wonderful IHOP real quick!" Deputy Will joked.

"Thanks Will."

As we got our food, we tried to find an open area to sit and eat. Looking out the steel-mesh-barred window, the water level in the street didn't look that bad, maybe a foot or two high. Seasoned New Orleanians had seen more than that accumulate from a routine heavy rain. It was coming down in sheets and the wind had kicked up. The good news was the water level was nowhere near my dad's car or mine, and I was starting to think we might get lucky.

"Hey Son, can you get some salt or something? This tastes like crap!"

I had to laugh. "Yeah. Let me see what I can find. I told you that you should have left with Gladys and Norman (my aunt and uncle). You're eating prison food now."

"Just get me some salt, Son. I don't want to hear all that!"

"Calm down. Calm down. I'll find you something." The area

was really crowded, but there was no problem finding salt. "Here you go. Bon appétit."

"Bone what?" my dad asked, confused.

"Never mind. Enjoy your breakfast."

Afterward, he decided to stay and watch TV and I thought I would go up to the 10th floor and take a look at the city. The 10th floor is just high enough to get an expansive 360-degree view, except some of the view is obstructed by the small, reinforced windows.

As I stepped into the elevator, I noticed the floor was wet. The only other time I saw the elevator in this condition was when one of our crazy inmates got the brilliant idea to jump up and pull on a sprinkler system pipe that runs down the tier. It caused the water to explode out of the pipes and run down the elevator shaft, flooding the first two floors of the building.

When I got off the elevator on the 10th floor it had a few inches of water on it. Going to into the psych office, it looked like a tornado had demolished it. There was a big wooden board covering the hole where the air conditioning unit was. At about 5 a.m., the wind had blown the unit into the office and over the desk by the window. Nurse Donna was sitting in the middle of the mess.

Donna is a middle-aged black woman. She had worked at the jail, off and on, for over 12 years primarily as a psych nurse. She also has a mouth like a sailor. Donna had been resting her feet on the desk when the blustery winds blew the air condition unit into the psych office and nearly knocked her on the floor.

"Gavin, you should have seen that shit! That unit came flyin',
and then the rain followed right behind it," Donna said.

"You all right? You look a little wet."

"Ha ha, smart ass. Of course I'm wet. The rain was flying all
over the place. We were trying to cover the opening up with anything
we could get our hands on."

In the office, the copy machine, computers, psych papers, and
various other things were either wet or scattered on the ground. At
one point, Donna and Nurse Robert said they had to get out of the
office because the wind and rain were too strong. "Man, I slipped
and fell on my ass and everything! You should have seen it!" Donna
said.

"I would have paid big money to see that!"

"Screw you, Gavin! Screw you." She laughed about it and
talked about what went on the night before.

Around 11 a.m., the weather outside appeared to be improving.
Looking out one of the second-floor windows, the damage around
our building didn't look that bad. The water level outside appeared to
be between two and three feet and it seemed we were through most
of the storm. I was thinking maybe we had made it through okay.

Lunchtime was approaching, and I went to check on my dad.
He was lying down, listening to the radio and reading a magazine. I
asked him what he was reading and he said, "This is some kind of
fashion magazine."

I was a little surprised and asked, "Where did you get that?"

With a guilty look on his face, he pointed to his right and said, "Out of that bag over there." I turned to see what he was talking about, and about 15 feet from us was an open school bag.

A little stunned and angry, I asked, "Did you take that out of there, Dad?"

"Yeah, why?"

"You can't go looking through other people's stuff! You tryin' to get me in trouble or what?"

"No, don't worry. I was gonna put it back."

"Come on, Dad. Don't go looking in other people's stuff like that! You might really piss someone off. I don't need that right now. You're not at home."

"All right, all right. I'll put it back."

"Hurry up. Better yet, give it here and I'll do it." Now I knew my dad must really be bored and losing it to go looking through the bag of someone he doesn't even know — and reading a fashion magazine.

It made me think back to a story that gets told every year at my Aunt Gladys and Uncle Norman's house during Christmas dinner. Both my dad and my uncle were in World War II in Reims, France. Both men were musicians, but my dad was in the Army band, and my uncle was fighting in the war. My dad played saxophone and clarinet and my uncle played trumpet. They didn't know each other until one fateful day, when my dad sat on my Uncle Norman's bunk and was looking through Norman's mail.

Enraged, Norman asked, "What the hell are you doing?"

My dad, just being his usual self said, "You're from New Orleans? So am I!"

As the story goes, Uncle Norman shot back, "What the hell does that have to do with you looking through my mail?"

"I have a sister back in New Orleans who I'd like to set you up with when you get back home." Norman immediately thought to himself, *Great; this guy's trying to set me up with his fat, ugly sister.* He did agree to meet my dad's sister, and when he went to the door to pick her up he was amazed to see how beautiful she was.

"Gavin let me tell you, your Aunt Gladys had the most beautiful tanned body I had ever seen and it was LOVE at first sight!" And they have been together ever since. They recently celebrated their 60th wedding anniversary.

That's a glimpse into the mind of my dear old dad.

At about 3:15 p.m., I went up to the 10th floor to go to work, performing my nursing duties. I told my dad I'd see him later and to stay out of trouble. I felt funny saying that because it was like warning a kid or something. When I got up there, I got a report from the day nurse; that's when the fun really started. One of our "regular" arrestees, J.W., had hurt himself.

He's a white male, about 30 years old, with a multitude of psychiatric illnesses. I really can't completely describe J.W., but I'll try. He is, by far, the most bizarre, out-of-touch with reality person with whom I have ever come in contact. No one knows where he is from or if he has any family. He's thin and stands about 5' 8". He's missing his two front teeth, has greasy light brown hair and pasty white skin, and speaks with an accent like a 10-year-old country boy. He has multiple personalities: One day he thinks he's Elvis Presley and the next day he is calling me "Dad" or, "Hey Jim, you're my brother." Sometimes he thinks he's Kurt Cobain (from the rock band Nirvana), and at other times he thinks he's George W. Bush.

J.W. was on the floor that day, playing in the water that had come in when the air conditioning unit blew into the office. While frolicking, he slipped and hit his head on his cell's toilet, cutting his skull wide open. It required a dozen stitches to close.

The doctor ordered "neuro checks Q1 X 24." That meant we had to check his vital signs every hour and make sure his eyes would properly react to light. We also were to ask him some basic questions, like his name and the date, even the name of the current president of the United States. With his mental condition, J.W. might say anything on any given day, so this part of the test wasn't much good.

The first check was all right, but during the second one J.W. looked really pale and said, "I'm real dizzy." His blood pressure was dangerously low, and his pulse was racing. Both were potentially very risky and needed immediate attention, especially the blood pressure. I notified the doctor on call at one of the other facilities, and he ordered a saline water I.V. to pump fluid directly into J.W.'s veins in order to bring up his blood pressure and lower his pulse rate — STAT. The main problem was we were dealing with a psychiatric inmate who lacked reason, common sense, and a normal understanding of reality. He might not understand we were trying to help him with the treatment.

Having dealt with J.W. on a regular basis for the past few years, I had developed a pretty good rapport with him.

"Hey Dad I don't feel good ... I think I'm gonna pass out," he said to me.

"J.W., when was the last time you ate or drank anything?" I asked.

"I don't know, but I'm hungry, Dad."

"All right, J.W., can you walk up to the front so I can get you something to drink?"

"Sure thing, Daddy!"

I walked briskly to the back storage room, making sure not to slip and fall, and I got a PowerAde drink for him out of the refrigerator.

"Hold still, all right? I need to start an I.V. on you."

As he began to drink the PowerAde, I went to the medical supply room to get the needed intravenous supplies, then returned.

"Why are you doing that, Dad?"

"J.W., I'm not your dad. Now sit still."

"Don't say that, Dad; please. What are you doing? Don't! That hurts!"

"J.W., sit still and shut up!"

At this point, I could see that this was going to be a problem, and I called the second floor to get another nurse to help me. In addition to dealing with this situation, the rest of the inmates on the floor were yelling for food, medications, and to change the channel on the television. The storm was picking back up, the atmosphere was getting frenzied.

After a few minutes, Nurse Urban showed up, to my relief.

"What seems to be the problem?" he asked.

"J.W.'s blood pressure is about 50/30 and his pulse is quite elevated. I called the doctor and he wants an I.V. STAT. He keeps moving all over the damn place."

We convinced J.W. to lie down on a bench to help restrict his movement.

"Hey Gavin, hold his shoulder down while I try his other arm."

"Dad, what the hell are y'all doin'? That hurts. Stop!"

As we were tending to him, I looked down the tier and saw two inmates fighting.

"Hang on a second. Let me go get some deputies to break up that fight in the back!" I said.

Running down the central walkway, I slipped on some water and almost fell flat on my butt. I was able to catch the door and regain my balance before I fell in all the water. After notifying Security of the fight, I returned to try and get the I.V. started. Checking his blood pressure again, I was unable to get a diastolic reading.

This was about to be a critical situation. Although J.W. didn't know it, his condition was life-threatening.

Normally when someone is in a condition this bad we would route him or her to a hospital by ambulance, but that was not an option. With the streets flooded and the storm raging, we had to make do. Even though he was not a contributing member of society, it was our job as nurses and employees of the Criminal Sheriff's Office to do everything we could for him as we would do for anyone in our custody.

"Stop now! I can't take it anymore!" J.W. screamed.

With our frustration mounting, we decided to take a break.

In his country boy twang, J.W. said, "Thanks Dad. Please don't do that anymore."

"Listen, J.W., just stay still, lie down, and keep quiet. Got it?" Then I told Urban we should get a couple of the other nurses up here to give us a hand.

At this point, the fight I mentioned had resulted in one of the inmates having a cut above his right eye that needed stitches.

"Call Dr. Marcus and let him know that we've got someone who needs stitches," I told Urban.

"Don't you remember? The doctors are all in other buildings," he replied. "We have none here."

"Oh, man! You gotta be kidding." I decided to clean and cover the inmate's cut until he could see a doctor.

"Hey, I'm going to get a couple of nurses to help us," I said. As I made my way to the elevator, I could hear the females in the psychiatric ward whooping and hollering for their medicines.

"Hey all you mother fuckin' nurses and deputies, give us our damn medicine!" a female prisoner yelled. To make matters worse, the disciplinary females were on the opposite side of the psych females, egging them on.

"Y'all bitches are gonna die up in here!"

"Yeah, that's right!"

The situation was getting ugly real quick.

It seemed like an eternity while I waited for the elevator, and then I heard a voice over the intercom, "Hey Gavin, the elevator ain't working. You're gonna have to take the stairs."

Making my way to the stairwell, I looked out the window and could see three buildings in Mid-City ablaze. A piece of the sun showed itself behind the clouds. It appeared the storm was just about over.

The sun hadn't even set when the sound of gunfire crackled off in the distance. I didn't know what was going on, who was doing the shooting, or where it was coming from. The shots were sporadic and spread all over the city.

I made my way down the eight flights of stairs to the second floor to get some help with J.W. After locating two available nurses, I said, "Hey, can y'all come up to the 10th floor and help us with an I.V.? We're gonna have to hold him down while y'all try to stick him. The only problem is the elevator isn't working right now. We gotta take the stairs."

They reluctantly agreed. "I'm gonna go check on my dad real quick and then I'll be up there. Nurse Urban is already up there tryin' to keep J.W. calm," I explained to them. Then I left and made my way over to the little spot on the second floor where my dad and I were camped out.

"Hey Dad, what's up?" I could see he wasn't happy.

"What's up? Oh, I don't know. You tell me." It was obvious he was aggravated by the situation, but there was nothing I could do.

"I bet you wish you would have left, huh?"

"No kidding, Son."

"Hey, you don't have to get short with me. I told you to leave."

"Yeah, I know. I just want to take a shower!"

"That makes two of us. Hey, did you get something to eat? I got some canned goods if you want to heat something up in the microwave," I said, pointing toward the break room.

"What do you have?"

"Take a look in that little green bag right there." I asked one of the other nurses' mothers if she wouldn't mind taking my dad to the break room to help him heat his food.

I washed my face real quick in the community bathroom and then took the stairs back to the 10th floor to see what we could do with J.W. I stopped on the eighth floor to catch my breath, and I could hear the rattling of the bars and menacing chants from the inmates. Once I got to the 10th floor and made a turn off the stairwell, there was a nurse sitting on the floor getting medical assistance. A little stunned and confused, I asked, "What the hell happened?"

Evidently she had asthma and had aggravated her condition by taking the stairs from the second floor to the 10th floor. As if she was on her last breath she struggled to say, "I'm ... hum ... gonna, gonna ... be ... all ... all ... all right."

Right behind her, J.W. saw me and said, "Hey Dad. You back? Where you been?"

I replied, "Hey, Son, I'm here. You being a good boy?" Everyone began to laugh, putting the bizarre and deteriorating situation on hold.

"Yeah, Dad. Can I have something to eat? I'm starving."

"After we get this I.V. started you can eat."

"No, dammit! I want to eat now."

"Well, Son, you're gonna have to wait a little longer." I heard a few more chuckles from the background.

He lunged at me, "Goddammit, I want to eat!"

"You better sit the hell down now! Now! Now, J.W. Now!" I shouted.

Urban grabbed him from behind with a full-nelson move and sat him on the bench. After a minute or two of calming him down, we took some more vital signs; they were still not good.

His blood pressure was still dangerously low, and his heart was beating dangerously hard. He appeared all right and feisty on the outside, but internally he was in a lot of trouble.

With his vital signs at those levels for any length of time, he could go into heart failure and die. Nurse Yolanda was starting to catch her breath and said, "Y'all stand back. Let me see if I can start an I.V. on this crazy sonofabitch!"

In a joking manner, I jumped back and told J.W., "Look, you done pissed off your mother now. You're gonna be grounded!"

It was perhaps odd that on the brink of our first possible fatality, I tried to find a second or two to lighten the mood; but we were all focused on saving his life.

The nurse said, "Hold him still; give me a 20-gauge needle. Gavin, hold his feet and legs still and you, Favis, get that line ready to go."

J.W.'s eyes got real wide and a look of terror overcame his face. "What the hell are y'all doin' to me? No! Stop! No!" The toughest part was the fact that since J.W. is crazy — literally — we could not reason with him and make him understand we were trying to save his life.

"Listen J.W., please work with us," I said. "Be still and calm. We are trying to help you. Your life is in danger."

"No! Stop! Gimmie somethin' to eat!"

"Fuck it! Hold him still ... I'm going to stick him!" With that, my asthmatic colleague tried five different veins with no success. All the while, J.W. screamed and cried like a 10-year-old child. After about 15 minutes J.W.'s arms looked like pincushions, so we decided to call the medical director to see what he wanted told do. Charity

Hospital is about a mile from our building, and by that time, we were surrounded by about four to six feet of water.

Although the weather was clearing, it was still unsafe out there. We had no way of knowing Charity was barely functioning, and wouldn't have been able to help anyway.

After getting word to the medical director through a deputy, and then a ranking official, we were told to bring J.W. to the second floor and he was going to swim over — yes, swim — from IPC (Intake Processing Center). I heard from a couple of deputies they tried to build a dam near the entrance to our building, but those attempts were unsuccessful.

"I'll be there as soon as I can. Try to calm him down and take his vital signs every five minutes until I get there," the medical director said. A deputy was called to the medical office and asked to secure J.W. so we could bring him to the second floor via the stairwell. As we were getting ready to go someone asked sarcastically, "Where are we bringing Elvis? To Graceland or what?"

Again, we had a few laughs. J.W. innocently asked, "We goin' home, Dad?"

At this point, I wanted to keep him as calm as possible, so I replied, "If you're a good boy we might. Just cooperate with us and we'll see."

"That's great, Dad! I'll be good, I promise. I Promise!"

And with that, we handcuffed J.W. and slowly walked him down the hot, muggy, stairwell — carefully, *very* carefully.

Chapter Two

BY NOW IT WAS ABOUT 8 P.M. OR SO, and I hadn't talked to my dad in a while. I asked another nurse to stay with J.W. for a few minutes so I could check on him. After going to the break room and finding the television not working, I went to the west side of the second floor to see who was over there. After surveying the area for a few seconds, I asked, "Anybody seen my dad?" A couple deputies said he was over on the south side listening to the radio with some other families. "Thanks guys. See ya later."

While heading to the south side, I overheard someone say the storm completely demolished the Twin Span bridges. Those bridges, each about five miles long, connect eastern New Orleans to the suburb of Slidell across a narrow section of Lake Pontchartrain. The "twin spans," as locals call them, are a vital link between the city and eastern and northern suburbs. I couldn't believe it. Entire sections of the bridges just plain gone. It sounded too incredible to believe. If the destruction I was hearing about was true, I wondered if other bridges throughout the city were damaged as well.

When I found my dad, he was playing cards with three deputies and a couple other guys. I didn't know exactly how to approach the situation.

After a few minutes of taking in this scene, I softly asked,

"What's up, Dad?"

Looking a bit surprised to see me, he said, "Uh ... just playing cards and listening to the radio, Son."

"Did you eat any dinner?"

"Yeah, I had some kind of stew with chicken in it ... it was okay."

"You been taking your medicine?" I asked.

"Oh yes, Son! I only have about five blood pressure pills left," he said while lighting up a cigarette.

"I'll go upstairs later and see if we have any. We have someone who's sick who we're tryin' to take care of. I'll talk to you later."

"All right, Son. See you later."

As I started to walk away, the deputies said, "We'll keep an eye on him." I thanked them and went back to my duties.

I hoped Dad wasn't playing cards for any money, although money wouldn't have done him any good in there. Walking back toward the second floor clinic, I spotted Dr. Inglese trying to dry off with paper towels. With a little smile, I asked, "A little wet out there, huh?"

"Just a little, Gavin. Where's J.W.?"

"He should be in the back room of the second floor clinic. He thinks he's going back to Graceland."

With a puzzled look he asked, "What? Why would he think that?" Obviously, he was not too familiar with J.W.'s personality and with six or seven thousand inmates, why would he be?

"Well, today he thinks he's Elvis Presley. Tomorrow, if there is a tomorrow for him, he might be Kurt Cobain. You never know with J.W."

Smiling sternly, Dr. Inglese said, "Now Gavin, you know you're not supposed to acknowledge things like that with a mentally ill person."

"I know, but the situation was becoming very chaotic and he seemed to calm down a little when the subject of Graceland came up."

"How the hell did that come up anyway?" the doctor asked.

"Please, don't ask. Let's just go and see how he is."

The second floor clinic is a room with a few desks, computers, no air conditioning, fans everywhere, and two small medical rooms. J.W. was in the back room happily playing the air guitar while a couple of nurses checked his vital signs.

The doctor walked in and commanded, "Let me see his vitals." He began to read them out loud, as if he was speaking to himself. "At 8:05 p.m., blood pressure 64/33, pulse 118. At 8:15 p.m. 68/37, pulse 116. At 8:25 p.m. 70/40, pulse 111."

It was now approaching 8:30 p.m. and the doctor wanted to take his own set of vital signs. "Somebody give me your blood pressure cuff and stethoscope." After taking the readings he announced, "Now he's 67/29 and pulse 114. How long has he been like this? We need to get him to Charity Hospital!"

Walking out of the room, the doctor tried to use his cell phone, which didn't work. Nearly all cell phone service in the New Orleans region had been knocked out by the storm. With the frustration mounting on his face, he blurted out, "Goddammit! I'll be back. I'm going to try and find Dr. Franks and Dr. Goddard and see if we can find a flat boat or something so we can get him to Charity!"

Meanwhile, I overheard some deputies talking about a ranking official in another building who had a heart attack, and many of the inmates were starting to riot. The situation continued to unravel.

"They're trying to burn down that mother fucker across the street," I heard a deputy telling another deputy.

"They got rank and deputies fallin' out over there!"

"This is getting fucked up around here!"

I went over to the narrow window to see if I could look down the street. It was pitch black, but catty-corner from our building, a fire burned brightly, lighting a tier on the third floor of one of the Templeman buildings.

A half -hour later, we'd received no word from the doctor. I could barely make out the water level outside the building, but I couldn't see my car or my dad's. I grabbed a flashlight from one of the deputies and shined it in the direction of our cars, hoping to see if they were flooded. They looked all right — so far.

I went to find my dad and let him know the good news. Making my way back to our spot, I found him listening to the radio with a deputy and her boyfriend. They had set up their stuff next to us.

"Done playing cards?"

"Yeah, I was getting tired."

"Are you feeling all right?"

"Yeah, just tired. ..."

"I'll get off of work in a couple of hours. Do you need anything?"

"You got any chocolate or candy?"

What is the deal with old people and sweets? Laughing a little, I said, "No, but I'll ask around and see if I can find you some. I'll see you later."

"I've got a Twix bar if you want it," a female deputy whispered to me.

She put it in my hand without my dad seeing her do it. I said, "Here you go, Dad!"

Befuddled, he asked, "How did you get one that fast?" It's always a little bit of fun to fool old folks and children.

"Magic, Dad. Magic!" Turning back to her, I whispered,

"Thanks. I'll give you one back later."

With half a laugh and a smile, in a hushed voice she said, "Don't worry about it Gavin. We'll keep an eye on your dad."

"Thanks a lot," I softly replied. "Hey Dad, I'll be back in a couple of hours."

With his mouth half-full of the candy bar, he said, "Okay, Son. See you later. "

Over by the second floor clinic, I saw the three doctors

huddled together talking. I could only assume they were trying to decide what to do about our Elvis.

"Hey guys, what's up?" I asked.

"Well, we're working on getting a boat. We have a ranking officer and a deputy over at one of the other buildings who are both having medical problems, so we may have to bring all three in a boat to Charity."

"I hate to mention it, but we have another inmate on the 10th floor who got into a fight and has a cut above his left eye," I said.

"How bad is it?" one of the doctors asked. He had a demonstrative "here we go again" look on his face.

"I Steri-Stripped it and covered it. He could probably use three to five stitches." Steri-Strips are generally used to keep a laceration intact until a doctor can look at it and stitch it up. Or, if the cut is small enough, it can be used to help it close and heal.

"Oh, great. Somebody find Dr. Marcus and get him to go check the wound and do the stitches, if necessary," Dr. Inglese said.

"I'll go find him and go up to 10. Y'all gonna take care of J.W.?" I asked.

"We've got it. Go ahead." With that, I started to ask around to see if anyone knew where Dr. Marcus was.

I eventually found him and a nurse on the fourth floor treating an inmate who was having an asthma attack. I could barely see because it was so dark. The doctor was dealing with about as much as he could handle and I hated to say anything. "Hey, Doc. What's going on here?"

Looking very tired, he said, "We're treating this guy for asthma. We're about to take him to the second floor for a breathing treatment. What's going on with you?"

"We've got a guy on 10 who might need some stitches."

"When I'm done here I'll be up there. Give me a couple of minutes."

"All right. I'm heading up now."

The stairwell was hot and muggy, but the inmate chanting seemed to have slowed down. Making my way up the stairs, it hit me that I hadn't spoken to my wife since the previous afternoon. Lora and I had only been married a couple years, and when we were apart, we tried to talk to each other as much as possible. With the situation rapidly deteriorating, I was desperate to talk with her.

The 10th floor phone system was still working at that point, and I hurried up the stairs to call her cell phone. Of course, the call didn't go through. I grabbed my wallet to look for the number of the hotel in Tyler, Texas, where she was staying. After a couple busy signals, the call finally went through, and I got the hotel operator.

"I need room 107, I think."

"Hold, please."

After a half-dozen rings there was no answer, so I hung up. As I was looking for Debbie's (my sister-in-law) number, my cell phone rang. It was Lora, thank goodness.

"Hey, babe. Is everything all right?" she asked.

Still catching my breath from climbing up the stairs I replied, "Well, I'm alive. It's been crazy around here. The inmates are shaking the bars, chanting, fighting and getting rowdy. We've got a guy who might be dying; there's water everywhere on the 10th floor; I heard a deputy might have had a heart attack; a nurse had an asthma attack; we got ..."

"Hey, hey, slow down a minute. Are *you* okay, Gavin?"

Breathing deeply, I said, "Yeah, I'm ... good ... ah ... just a little out of breath."

"Why?"

"Well, the elevators aren't working, so I have ... to go up and down the... stairs from ten to two and other floors in between... between all the madness and checking on my dad. I'm getting tired of running these stairs."

"You better slow down. I don't want anything to happen to you."

"I'll be all right. Hey listen, the phones are probably going to go out, so if I can't get through to you, that's the reason."

After an extended silence, Lora said, "I love you baby ... be ... safe. ..."

I could hear her voice cracking a little, which gave me a lump in my throat. "I'll be all right. Take care. Kiss the dogs, say 'hi' to everyone for me, and don't worry. I think the storm has passed. Oh yeah, I almost forgot, it looks like our cars avoided the flood waters.

There's about three to four feet of water surrounding our buildings, but our cars are in the highest spot in the parking lot."

With some hesitation in her voice, she said, "Th ... that's great. Hopefully, you'll be able ... to ... leave ... soon." I could tell she was beginning to cry.

"Are you crying? Please don't ... I'll be fine, " I reassured her. "What ...about your dad?"

"So far, he's all right. I think he now realizes he should have left. The only bad thing is he's running out of medicine."

"Hopefully, y'all won't be there too long."

I tried to be strong. "That would be nice. I'm just wondering how long it's gonna take for this water to go down. Anyway, I better get going. I love you. Take care and I'll talk to you soon."

"Bye, baby ... I love you ... so much. Miss you."

"Love you. Miss you too. Bye-bye."

Hanging up the phone, I could hear the female inmates yelling. The deputies appeared to be nowhere in sight. Walking over there and trying not to slip and fall with all the water on the floor, I heard someone say, "Who's there?"

Startled, I answered, "It's Nurse Johnson. Who's that?"
"Dr. Singh," the feminine voice replied with her foreign accent.

"Oh, hey, Dr. Singh. I heard these crazy women screaming and hollering over there and I came to see what was going on with them."

Dr. Singh is one of our psychiatrists and she was on the 10th floor, sleeping on a cot in the back office. "Hello Nurse Johnson. I was just taking a nap in the back and I heard the screaming also. What's going on?"

"I have no idea. I don't see any deputies anywhere. I'm gonna go down the tier and see what the problem is."

As nurses, we're not supposed to open any of the security gates. Since there were no deputies around, and there was someone screaming, I took it upon myself to open the gate to see what the problem was.

"What's wrong? Who's screaming down there?"

A female voice yelled, "The girl in my cell is having a seizure or somethin'!"

After popping the gate open, I carefully ran down the slippery hallway to see a twitching and unconscious female on the cell floor. She was unresponsive to my questions.

"How long has she been like this?"

"Man, I don't know. Five minutes maybe or somethin' like that."

I walked back to open the cell, which I obviously wasn't supposed to do, but I had no choice. I entered with Dr. Singh looking over my shoulder.

I said, "All right, I'm gonna roll her on her side. I'm going to need you to keep her on her side while I go get some help, all right?"

With some hesitation, the inmate replied, "Yeah, yeah, all right, man!"

Rushing to the medical office, I got a wheelchair and some ammonia capsules (sometimes called smelling salts), which are used to help someone wake up, and we often use them to see if an inmate is faking a seizure as they sometimes do — *imagine that!*

If someone is faking it, which happens quite a bit in the incarcerated environment, the person will react as if bleach or something like that was stuck up his or her nose. People having real seizure s will be unresponsive or slow to respond, and their eyes may roll back in their heads. They may also urinate or defecate on themselves.

By the time I got back she was somewhat responsive, and after I put the ammonia capsule under her nose she started to speak.

"What the fuck? SHIT! What the hell is that shit, man?!"
I asked, "You feelin' all right? Stay still and let me get some vital signs on you."

Her blood pressure was 134/85 and her pulse was 110. Respirations were 18 per minute (borderline elevated)and her temperature was 99. Based on the vital signs, which were pretty normal, she may or may not have had a seizure. I began asking her a series of questions that could help me determine whether she was being honest or not.

"Do you have seizure disorder?"

"Yeah, I have 'caesars,'" she pronounced it.

"What do you take for your seizures?"

"I take them Dilantin 100s and Phenobarbital 30s," she replied, referring to the dosages.

"When was the last time you took your meds?"

"Well, I just got arrested two days ago and these bitches around here won't give me my meds. I guess I took them about a week ago."

"A week ago? If you've only been in jail for two days and your last meds were a week ago, what happened to the five days in between?"

"Well, you know ... I don't know man ... I was partying before I came to jail."

"Were you doing any drugs before you came to jail?"

A devilish smile came over her face and she looked me straight in the eye and said, "No sir! Not me!"

Obviously, I couldn't believe that part of her story, so I countered, "Yeah, right. So if we did a drug test it would show up negative, right?"

"Why you givin' me a hard time now, man? You gonna help me or what?"

"Yes. Get in this wheelchair so I can bring you to the office."

One of the requirements of the medical field is that everything that happens to patients or, in this case, inmates, has to be documented. We, as nurses, have to write nurses' notes, usually with vital signs and the time and date the incidents occur, along with detailed descriptions of what happened. In hospitals, this is essential because people are in the hospital because they are sick. In a correctional facility, inmates usually are not sick initially, but when something happens, a nurse is still expected to document it. Workers in the medical field are always open to lawsuits, and if things are not documented, a lawyer can use that against us.

Most occurrences in a corrections setting are not life-threatening, but the area I work in — psychiatry — is unique. People often try to kill themselves when they are in jail, so we take every threat seriously. If someone wants to take his or her own life, we don't want it to happen in jail. We have to protect those people from themselves as well as others. In this case, we had someone who may or may not have had a seizure. If I didn't document what happened and report it to a doctor, then I would not be doing my job.

Everything that happened earlier with J.W. and the other medical incidents had to be documented. Those people often cry wolf, yet we take every incident as if it were a true medical crisis.

I brought the woman to the medical office, and Dr. Marcus and a nurse walked in at the same time. "Where's the guy with the laceration?" the doctor inquired.

Trying to compose myself a bit, I said, "Give me a minute, Doc. I have this female inmate here who may have had a seizure. She said she takes Dilantin and Phenobarbital, but hasn't taken her medication in a week. Can I get an order for both?"

Looking fatigued he said, "Yeah. Get me her chart, and I'll

write an order. In the meantime, give her a loading dose of 400 mg of Dilantin now, another 300 mg in four hours, and another 200 mg in another four hours."

"Okay, Doc. Thanks."

The inmate was stable enough to walk, so I gave her the medication and got one more set of vital signs — for documentation purposes — and walked her back to her cell. I was now playing nurse and deputy. After locking her cell, it seemed like every female all of a sudden had a problem.

"Come here, white boy!"

"My head hurts! Damn!"

"I'm in pain! You gotta help me!"

Walking off the tier, I had to ignore all the yelling and screaming about headaches and back pain and other feigned maladies. I called down to the Watch Commander's office. After a few rings, someone picked up the phone and with some frustration in my voice, I asked, "Will y'all send a deputy or somebody up to 10? The doctor is up here, and we have somebody who needs stitches."

"Who the hell is this?" grumbled the unfamiliar voice.

"Nurse Gavin. There's no deputy up here and we need one ASAP!"

"No deputy? Hang on. We'll have one up there in a minute." I knew this would take a while because the elevators were out. There aren't too many deputies who will feel like walking up eight flights of stairs in the heat.

"Hey, Dr. M., you ever see so much stuff goin' on at one time?" I asked.

Looking at me and half-heartedly smiling, he said, "No, I can't say I have. This is pretty wild!"

Deciding to make small talk, I offered, "Did you hear about the Twin Spans? I heard they're totally destroyed."

"What? You kidding?" The smile melted from his face.

Pointing to the radio in the other office, I said, "That's what WWL (local station 870 AM, our only news source during and after the storm) said!" Immediately following the hurricane and for weeks afterward, most of the city's radio stations combined their resources and personnel into a single 24-hour broadcast on multiple frequencies, both AM and FM. We only got one reporting source, and the facts and details were often confusing. Sometimes, we heard gut-wrenching, heart-breaking pleas for help from stranded residents.

"That's unbelievable," the doctor replied. "I wonder if the other roadways are damaged too."

"I don't know, I only heard about the Twin Spans."

"Where's this guy with the laceration above his eye?"

"I had to call downstairs to get Rank to send up a deputy. We're security-free up here."

"Oh, that's just great."

Dr. Marcus then stood up and looked around for a second or two and asked, "Is there an outside phone line that works up here?"

"Yeah. Try that phone in the office over there."

"I'll be right back."

Meanwhile, I saw Nurse Favis on her cell phone in the corner of the soaked office, looking out the window as she spoke.

"Hey Favis, you can go back downstairs if you want. I got it up here," I said.

"You sure?"

"Yeah. When you go down, pass by the Watch Office and tell them the doctor is up here and we need a deputy up here, please."

"No problem. See you later."

It was about 10:45 p.m., and it was starting to calm down a little bit inside the prison. I could hear a few arguments and inmates being loud, but that was common on the 10th floor. Normally, I could close the door and turn on the air conditioning. Since the air conditioner was now sitting on the floor, that wasn't an option. With no a/c, and all the moisture and puddles on the floor, this office was the last place I wanted to be. Taking a walk around to the south side of the 10th floor, I decided to look out of one of the small windows.

It was so dark inside it looked like I was in a closed closet with the light off. It was spooky to see nothing but darkness outside and various buildings on fire. The fires were scattered all over as far as I could see. I could barely see a small part of what appeared to be the moon. Faint traces of clouds floated by, but no rain. At that moment, a part of me couldn't wait for the morning to get a real idea of what it was going to look like around the city.

The House of Detention building I was in is 10 stories high.

The view includes parts of the Central Business District downtown, Uptown, and Mid-City during the daylight hours. I was feeling pretty confident our cars were still all right. Some of the employees parked on the street and the employee lot was full. The problem was the street, and front part of the employee lot are quite low. Most of New Orleans is below sea level, and elevations are often spoken of in inches, rather than feet. Inches can make a difference when a heavy downpour floods the streets. I was sure those cars in the employee lot would be flooded or have at least a little water in them. The employee lot is a big one that holds 300 to 400 cars and has a pretty good slope to it. As I mentioned, we had parked in the highest possible spot, so if ours got flooded then all the other cars would already be under water.

I was mesmerized by a blazing fire that appeared to be near St. Charles Avenue, a majestic boulevard from Downtown to Uptown New Orleans, running past Tulane and Loyola universities.

Referred to by locals as simply, "the avenue," St. Charles is beautifully lined with majestic live oak trees and magnificent mansions, with streetcars rolling through the middle.

I heard footsteps coming up the stairs. The deputy had finally arrived. We could get those stitches done, and I could go back downstairs to get some sleep.

Breathlessly, the deputy said, "Y'all … got... someone … who's … cut. Damn, that's a long-ass haul up those steps!"

"Tell me about it. I've been walkin' those steps all day," I answered. "Do me a favor, go get H.B. on the south side, cell seven for me, please."

"Where do you want him?" he panted.

Pointing to my right, I said, "On the bench, right there. The doc is going to stitch him up real quick."

"All right. You got it, G."

Dr. Marcus was still on the phone, but he wasn't speaking. I waited for a minute or so before I said anything. "Doc, we've got the inmate ready for the stitches."

"All right, give me a minute." The inmate was cooperating, thank God, so I was able to remove the bandage easily to see how the cut looked. Dr. Marcus hung up the phone and took four or five steps toward us before slipping forward directly into the medicine cart was near us. Fortunately, he caught himself before he fell in the puddle of water that caused him to slip in the first place.

"Goddammit! What the hell? That would have capped my day off just right."

"Don't feel bad; I slipped at least two or three times today. This is an accident waiting to happen," I said.

The inmate with the laceration was also one of our regulars. He's a paranoid schizophrenic who is constantly getting into fights with other inmates, having a knack for hurting the hands of the inmates with his face. Surprisingly, he was calm at the time, so I hoped things would go smoothly.

"Gavin, please get me a small laceration kit, a number 4.0

Vicryl stitch, Lidocaine, and a five-eighth length needle," Dr. Marcus said.

"I'll be right back," I said, taking a mental note of his request. Our medical supply room is very small on the 10th floor and not well stocked. After looking for a few minutes, I realized we only had laceration kits and no stitches of any kind.

Exhausted and agitated, I said, "Hey Doc, I'm gonna have to go to the second floor clinic to get some stitches. I'll be back." Walking down the stairs, I tried to figure out how many times I'd been up and down them that day. All I knew was that I'd sleep well that night.

Chapter Three

THE SECOND-FLOOR CLINIC WAS GETTING NOISIER and noisier, filling up with employees' families who were moving out of the cafeteria area. There were some volatile people in there, and tempers were starting to flare. After navigating my way around the sleeping bags and mattresses on the floor, I was able to get to the medical supply room. A family was set up in there, blocking the cabinet where the stitches were kept. There were two small children sleeping, so I tip-toed around them and grabbed the box of stitches.

By this point, I was thirsty and hungry. Nurse Favis was eating a sandwich — which looked awfully good.

"Whatcha' eatin'?" I asked.

"Hot sausage sandwich. You want one?"

"Hell, yeah. You don't mind?"

"Gavin, you know you're my boy. I just got to cook it up right quick."

Right near the front of the clinic was a refrigerator and what looked like a little portable electric burner with a frying pan on top.

"Don't worry about it. I didn't know you had to cook it."

"That's all right, G; it'll only take a couple of minutes. What do you want on it? We got mayo, mustard, lettuce, and tomatoes."

"Everything, but tomatoes."

"Comin' right up!"

The loud sizzling and smell of sausage frying filled the room. I could hear people talking in the main corridor about the different things they were hearing on the radio about The Storm and its aftermath.

"You got somethin' to drink?" Favis asked.

"Nope; let me go over by my stuff. I have some water over there. I'll be right back," I said.

"I'll have your sandwich ready when you get back."

"Thanks."

The hallway was dimly lit, since we were running off of a diesel-powered generator and only a few lights were on to conserve energy. My dad was asleep and Deputy Jeanne's boyfriend was lying across from him, listening to the radio.

Grabbing my blue duffel bag and opening it up, I whispered, "I just came to get some water."

"That's cool. You been runnin' around all day, huh?" he asked.

Shaking my head and raising my eyebrows, I replied, "You have no idea. It's been crazy around here today. Thank God it's almost over." Opening up my bottle of water and taking a quick sip, I said, "I'll be back in a little while."

"Later G..."

"See ya."

After gobbling up the hot sausage sandwich, I made my way up the stairs once again. This time I brought a flashlight just in case.

When I got back to the 10th floor, I could hear someone hollering.

When is this crap gonna end?

Turning the corner, I saw a deputy holding the inmate who needed stitches face down on the floor with the doctor standing over him chuckling a little bit.

"What's wrong with this idiot?" I asked.

The deputy turned to me and said, "All of the sudden he started freakin' out and yelling, 'Don't kill me, Don't kill me.' Then he lunged at the doc."

Dr. Marcus smiled and nodded.

"Well, Doc, do you want to do these stitches or what?"

Darting his eye at me, he said, "Let him calm down a minute."

Before he could finish what he was saying, the psycho inmate started yelling, "Help me! Help me! Don't kill me please!" This went on for a few minutes. Finally, I was able to convince the inmate we were trying to help him.

"All right, let's get this over with," Dr. Marcus said. As he set up the Lidocaine(to deaden the cut), the inmate went berserk. "No, no! Stop, Please!"

At this point, Dr. Marcus shouted, "Fuck it! Get a medical refusal form and let's sign it! He is obviously not going to let me do anything! You can Steri-Strip the cut when he calms down. He's all right."

After we both signed the form and had the deputy sign it as a witness, I put it in his chart.

The doctor said he was leaving. "See ya later Dr. Marcus." I said apologetically.

"Bye."

The situation was wearing on him.

The inmate sat on the bench, rocking back and forth while staring at the floor. Mumbling to himself, he appeared to be calming down. "Harold, I'm going to cover your cut up, okay?" At first he didn't answer. I waited a second or two and tried again.

"Hey Harold, look up for me please!" He looked up. The deputy handcuffed him and sat him straight up.

Harold then very calmly said, "You may do as you please." His change in demeanor was a little freaky, but I Steri-Stripped his cut and covered it with a bandage.

After I was finished, the deputy put Harold back in his cell. Nurse Donna came through the door by the stairwell. She was obviously out of breath and sat down in the medical office. "Damn, that's a hot-ass stairwell! It took me 15 minutes to get up those damn stairs," she said, trying to catch her breath.

I smiled, "You want me to call the doctor? I can give you a breathing treatment if you need it."

Laughing back at me, she said, "Kiss my big black ass!"

I gave her a rundown of the evening's events, and she told me about some things she had heard on the radio. After leaving the 10th floor and walking the stairs for that last time that night, I thought about Lora and our puppies. Then it hit me that I also hadn't spoken to my mother in several days.

My mom works for Amtrak, and I didn't know if she had evacuated or not. She doesn't have a cell phone, so I couldn't call her. I thought I remembered her saying she was leaving over the weekend (before the hurricane) for Chicago on the City of New Orleans train.

My mother, Roberta, had come to New Orleans from Chicago for Mardi Gras when she was 19. She met my dad, at the time a jazz musician at the Blue Room. He was nearly 30 years her senior. He helped her through some difficult situations with a roommate and eventually they developed a relationship. Although they divorced when I was eight, my parents are still friends to this day.

My mom has another son, my younger half-brother, Alex, who is 19 and lives in the nearby coastal town of Waveland, Mississippi. I don't get to see him very often because he lives with his father and I hadn't talked to him in a while. I said a little prayer and hoped he was all right too. Many people were in my situation. Calls couldn't go in or out for the most part. The uncertainty was agonizing.

My family was on my mind as I walked the stairs with my flashlight on. Before I knew it, I had walked too far and found myself confused and standing in a stairwell just above the first floor level.

I pointed my flashlight down right below my feet and could see water, about a foot or so, just above the first step. Making my way back up to the second floor, I saw a female deputy walking with a towel around her head and a bottle of shampoo in her hand. Her "at home" presence was a stark contrast to the conditions.

As she turned the corner I asked, "Where can we take a shower?"

She acted like she didn't hear me because she kept walking. *Was I seeing things?*

I saw Deputy Henry by the side door to the Watch Office. "Hey Henry, can we take a shower somewhere?"

Looking both ways before saying anything, he whispered, "Get your stuff, come back here and you can take a shower."

Our things were not far away and as I approached the disorganized pile I was sure to be as quiet as I could so I didn't wake my dad. My bags were at the end of my air mattress and Dad's foot was touching the edge of one of them. Thankfully, he was sound asleep and snoring. I grabbed my towel, a change of clothes, and my shampoo. Deputy Henry was by the side door when I got back, and he opened it quickly, telling me to hurry up. Obviously, the shower was for the deputies only; not the medical staff.

"Thanks a lot. I'm dying for a shower," I said.

"Hey G, the only problem is there's no hot water."

"That's all right, I've been sweating all day; I could use a cold shower."

"No problem," he said.

The shower stall was tiny with a very small, drippy shower head. It was smelly, dark, and dingy. I turned on the water, and, surprisingly it came out in a fairly strong stream. The deputy wasn't kidding, the water was ice cold!

I put my flip-flops on and stepped into the shower. *"Ooh, ooh! Damn that's cold!"* It was like somebody pouring a pitcher of ice water on my head. I jumped out and stood there naked with tensed muscles and my head nearly frozen, then eased my way back into the shower. I quickly soaped up and shampooed my head, but it didn't lather well.

After the showering in record time, I got dressed and made my way back to my "comfy" air mattress. My dad was still sleeping soundly and it was fairly quiet. I checked my cell phone one more time and it read 12:05 a.m. Thinking we might be stranded a little while, I shut it off to conserve the battery and rolled over to try and sleep.

I could hear the sounds of assorted radios with newscasters talking about the aftermath of the storm. I listened to the grim reality of the surrounding area. Apparently, the storm took a slight turn to the east and the Gulfport-Biloxi, Mississippi area, about 60 miles east of New Orleans, took a direct hit. They had 30-foot storm surges from the Gulf that washed away entire blocks of waterfront houses.

That also meant Waveland had been hit hard, where my brother lives. He doesn't live far from the beach, so all I could hope for was that he evacuated. I knew my mother must have been very worried about him.

The announcer on the radio sounded very grim, "... the Twin Span bridges are gone ... Destroyed! The city of Slidell, Louisiana, is inundated with water .... Massive devastation! We have word that the Gulf Coast region of Mississippi is obliterated. Gone! Some estimates have the storm surge as high as 50 feet ... We have reports that some of the levees in New Orleans have given way ... the pumps have failed ... there are **dead bodies** floating in the streets of the city. Dogs running wild. People are calling from their attics pleading for help ..."

I listened for a half-hour or so. With each passing moment, the sinking feeling in my stomach got deeper and deeper. It looked like we were going to be stuck there a while. Taking one last look at my dad, I rolled over again and said another little prayer. What would be next?

Chapter Four

I WOKE IN THE DARKNESS AROUND 5 A.M. to my dad rummaging through his duffel bag. It felt like I had just laid my head down to sleep.

Whatcha' lookin' for, Dad?"

"My medicine. I can't see real good ... You got a flashlight?"

Lying on the other side of us was Nurse Urban and his mother. This lady was a piece of work. I would come to appreciate the things she would do as the time went by.

Urban must have heard my dad. "Mr. Johnson, I have a flashlight for you. Here you go."

"Oh, thank you." My dad leaned over and whispered close to my left ear, "I gotta' take a dump!"

Realizing it would be dark in the bathroom, I told him I would go with him. It was only about 25 feet from where we were set up. Everybody in our section of the building used this bathroom and, up until this point, it still worked.

Whispering, I said, "Dad, give me the flashlight, put your hand on my shoulder and follow me.

Once we got to the bathroom, we saw that it was pretty dark and starting to smell like a foul public toilet.

"Dad, make sure you clean the seat before you sit."

"Yeah, I got it."

After a couple of audible gaseous emissions, I could hear him straining a little.

"I think I'm constipated Son. I don't have my Sun-Chlorella pills – I forgot them when I was packing. They help me go to the bathroom and keep me young." In the past, he had told me about those pills. He swears they make him look and feel younger.

"I thought those were the pills that make you look younger; I didn't know they were a laxative too."

"Everybody I meet can't believe that I'm 83 — they think I'm 50 to 55 years old!"

"Come on Dad, 50 years old?"

"I'm telling you Son. These pills do all kinds of things for me." After a couple more unpleasant, but funny, sounds, he said, "Y'all got anything to help me go?"

Trying not to laugh, I said, "We should. Do you want me to look now?"

"No. Later." With that, he buckled up and we went back to bed. After fumbling around in the dark, I said, "Wait here and I'll be right back."

The second-floor clinic was dark and very quiet. There were people lying just about everywhere on the floor. The medicine carts were in the back, of course, so I once again tiptoed around everyone on the floor. The carts were full of just about everything a medical staff person could need. People who are incarcerated often get better medical treatment than they would get if they weren't in jail.

Anyway, one of the nurses heard me. "Who's there? What are you looking for?"

"It's Gavin. My dad needs a laxative."

"Look in the bottom right-hand drawer. There's some magnesium citrate. That'll help him." Procedures were out the window at this point. We were keeping the medicine secure from having a free-for-all, but survival was the name of the game. My dad's health was definitely priority.

"Thanks."

I decided to go to the break room to see the water level outside the building. The visibility was poor, but I could see the rising waters were getting closer to our cars. Some cars were already almost completely covered, but ours still appeared to be safe. *How deep could this get?*

It was daybreak and looking like it was going to be a nice day. The sun was just starting to shine and, amazingly, there were no clouds. Walking back over by my dad, I noticed there were a few people moving around, but for the most part everyone was still asleep. I walked over by the front entrance and saw Nurse Cecilia and her family talking.

"Hey Gavin, what's going on?"

"Nothing much. Looks like we survived another storm."

"I guess so ..."

In her Southern drawl she asked, "How's your daddy?"

"He seems to be okay. I'm sure he wishes he would have evacuated."

In unison, four members of her family and Cecilia all said, "Us too!"

After some laughter, Cecilia asked, "You heard about them levees?"

"I heard something on the radio about them failing or something. Why? What did you hear?" I asked.

"Oh yeah, I heard over by Lake Pontchartrain and also Chalmette (a suburb of New Orleans to the southeast of the city, where Cecilia lives) was fillin' up with water."

"You heard anything about Kenner?" I was worried about my home.

"Not yet, but if I do I'll let you know ... if you're hungry, I heard they're makin' some breakfast over by the kitchen."

"All right, thanks. See you later."

It was about 6:30 a.m. or so, and I left to see if they really were making breakfast. It sure sounded good. The break room was starting to get a few stragglers, and just about everyone was taking turns looking out of the window. It seemed everyone, like me, wanted to see if his or her cars were flooded or not.

"Aw, Jesus, man. My car is gone!" someone yelled out.

"Don't feel bad — mine too," another voice echoed from the back of the room. The consensus seemed to be that everyone's car had taken some water.

Patiently waiting my turn, I saw the water was touching my dad's car tire, about a quarter of the way up. Mine was parked right next to his with the water barely touching my tire. I was feeling pretty good that our cars were safe, since the storm was gone and the skies looked like they would be clear for the day. Looking to my right, I could see about three or four cars with the back windows blown out or shattered. I overheard someone say they saw the wind blow parts of the exhaust vents off the Templeman buildings, a couple of the main buildings within the local penal system, that landed on those cars, smashing out some of the back windows. Since those cars were in the back of the parking lot, they had survived the initial flooding, but not the flying vents. The parking lot was beginning to look like a big dirty swimming pool, with hundreds of flooded cars in it. Some of the cars had started to float about.

It was about this time one of the ranking officials came in and said, "Breakfast will be served between 7:30 and eight in the old cafeteria area." Some people immediately left to get in line, while others rushed to notify their families breakfast was about to be served. Instead of rushing, I took my time to get my dad. I figured I'd let him sleep a little longer.

It was close to eight o'clock. I was reading one of my books while lying on my mattress when my father woke up. "Hey Dad, you want some breakfast?"

"Yeah, what do they have?"

"I don't know. We have to grab a plate over near the old cafeteria and get in line. Come on, it'll be like Piccadilly's." Piccadilly's is a Southern cafeteria chain my father lists as one of his favorites.

Looking a little confused he said, "Hold on a second, let me put on my shoes."

The line was long and filled with all kinds of characters — young, old, big, small, black, white, yellow, and everything in between. During the night, they must have hung a tarp to separate the cafeteria from the kitchen. Looking at some of the passersby, I could see they were serving runny oatmeal, a bright red hot dog, and a hard-boiled egg. It was readily apparent this was not going to be a very tasty breakfast. "Well, Dad, this won't be McDonald's, but it'll have to do."

"That's all right, Son. I'm hungry."

The line slowly moved along and after 10 minutes or so, we got our food and went down the hallway to eat.

"How is it, Dad?"

"Not bad."

"You want my oatmeal? I'm not a big oatmeal eater."

"Sure, put it here," he said, pointing to an empty spot on his plate. As I slid the runny oatmeal off my plate, I saw others doing the same. The oatmeal didn't seem to be popular with the young people. I concluded oatmeal, in general, is for the older generation. Good roughage, lowers your cholesterol or something.

Prisoners of Katrina

After breakfast, I gave my dad a few swigs of the magnesium citrate. "This should do the trick. Give it a couple of hours to work, all right?"

He nodded and said, "Where's the front door?" reaching in his pocket for a cigarette.

"Why? Do you want to smoke?"

"Well ... um ... I just want to get some fresh air."

I played along.

I had seen a few people the day before smoking by the front entrance to the building, but it was now under two feet of water.

"Wait here and I'll go find out."

I went to the Watch Commander's office. I was instructed to go by the inmate visitors' center, which is near the front entrance, but on the second floor. I went to go back and get my dad, but he was gone. I asked anyone who would listen, "Has anybody seen my dad?" A couple of people pointed toward the second-floor clinic. I went over there, but he wasn't there. I was walking toward the break room when I saw him coming out of the unisex bathroom. Agitated by now, I said, "I told you to wait and I'd be right back. You didn't smoke in that bathroom did you?"

"Yeah. Why? What's the big deal?"

"You're not at home. You can't just do whatever you want in here. This is a jail and if somebody sees you doing that then everybody will start doing what he or she wants, and we can't have that here. Come follow me, and I'll show you where to go next time."

I showed him the area where he needed to go to if he was going to smoke.

It's funny; for the last few years my dad has felt the need to try to hide the fact he smokes. He's been smoking for 50-plus years and had a mild stroke in 1998. When I go to visit him on my off days, he sometimes is smoking when I look through the window before I come in. When I come through the door, he cups the cigarette in his hand and plays dumb like a teenager, while smoke is coming from under his hand. Or he'll hear the door opening and get up and walk to the back of the house so I can't see him. I know what he's doing, but I go along with him. He knows I don't smoke, and I don't approve of him smoking, but I would never tell him what to do. I mean, he's made it to his 80s, right? I have to give him credit though; he has slacked off a bit, and he's definitely more aware of his health. The environment we were in was bad enough, so I couldn't really blame him for wanting a cigarette, and I could tell he was uncomfortable. I had tried to tell him what it was going to be like at the jail. If it was just me, it wouldn't be so bad, but having to keep track of him was stressing me out and creating tension between us. I didn't like treating him like a child, but I felt I needed to keep an eye on him.

"I'm gonna go up to the 10th floor to see how things are going." Jokingly, I added, "Stay out of trouble." He smiled and started to walk down to the visitors' area.

I told myself I would keep count of how many times I went up and down the stairs that day. Hopefully, it wouldn't be like the day before. Walking up the stairs, I took a look down from the second floor to the ground floor, and I could see that the water level was about halfway up the first set of stairs. I thought that was a little strange, since the storm was long gone. The water should have been receding, not rising. What I didn't know was that because of the levee breaks by Lake Pontchartrain, the entire city was filling up with millions of gallons of water, contaminated with oil, gas, sewage and rotting corpses.

The stairwell was really hot for so early in the morning, and I was going to make every effort to not make that hike if I could avoid it. The 10th floor was fairly calm when I got up there. I had forgotten we had taken in some St. Bernard Parish (a suburb adjacent to New Orleans) inmates and their deputies. They were housed on the 10th floor in the holding cell, an area about 20 by 25 feet. There were five or six deputies in there.

After observing the cramped situation, I decided to introduce myself. "Hey guys (there were actually a couple of females also), I'm Gavin, and I'm one of the nurses up here." They all introduced themselves and gave me a rundown of who was who and what they were there for.

"Make yourselves comfortable and if there's anything I can do, just let me know." A couple of nurses were in the waterlogged medical office, trying to clean up a little.

"What's up, y'all?" I asked.

In unison, they said, "Help!"

"Hold on just a minute," I replied.

Before I got started, I decided to try and call Lora. My cell phone had no signal, so I used the office phone. As you might imagine, the landline was dead too. I realized it would be a while before I would speak to her again.

I was really missing her. A lot.

I regretted going up there because for the next couple of hours, I was mopping up water and moving things around. After helping to clean up, I went back to the second floor to check on my dad. It was about 11 a.m., and it was getting hotter by the minute. There were two big fans set up in the middle corridor that circulated the hot, humid air, and the door was open in an attempt to cool the building.

Looking through the door, I could see water and what looked like raw sewage backing up through the drains in the recreation area outside. On a positive note, opening the door to the stairwell and having the fans on was helping with the air circulation and helped cool off the building somewhat. But they were also blowing the foul smells about.

My dad was near our area reading the newspaper from the weekend before the storm. I asked him if he was hungry, but he said he wasn't. With the stench around us, I wasn't really hungry either.

I decided to find somebody with a radio and ventured over to the right side of our area. I introduced myself to a young African-American man and his pregnant wife. "Hey, how are you doing? My name's Gavin. Do you mind if I listen to the radio with you?"

"Hey man, I'm T.C. and this is my wife. Have a seat," he said.

We got to talking, and I was quickly impressed with him. He said he just graduated from Loyola Law School, recently took the bar exam, and was headed into the Air Force as a lawyer. "I'm waiting to get my bar exam results, and then we're moving to Virginia."

I asked, "How do you think you did?"

"Oh, I feel pretty good about it man. I'm pretty confident I passed it. It *was* a bitch though."

"I bet. Now, how did you end up here?"

"My mom is Mrs. Chaisson. She works in the Watch Office."

It took me a second to realize who he was talking about, but then it hit me, "Oh, yeah, I know her."

It was about this time the radio announcer started talking about the levee breaks. "We have confirmation that there is a levee break at the Seventeenth Street Canal in Lakeview (an affluent area of New Orleans near Lake Pontchartrain). Also, levee breaks at the Industrial Canal in the lower Ninth Ward (a poor area of New Orleans). There is a failure at the London Street Canal and Chalmette is under 10 to 20 feet of water. I repeat, we have levee failures at ..."

Sitting down on the old, dirty floor I didn't know what to think. After a few seconds of reflection, I realized once again we were going to be stuck there for a while.

T.C. got up and paced around a little bit. "This is some bullshit, man."

"You ain't lying. I'll be right back. I'm gonna go tell my dad the bad news."

I went back over to where my dad was. Looking out the window at the water surrounding our building, I said, "Hey dad, it looks like we're going to be here a while."

A little confused, he asked, "We're not going home later? The storm is over isn't it?"

"Yeah the storm's over, but the levees have broken all over town. Water is pouring into the city."

"We're not close to any levees. We'll be able to leave later ..."

"Have you looked out the window lately? We're surrounded by water. We're not going anywhere!"

With a disturbed look, he asked, "How are our cars?"

"Come take a walk with me and I'll show you. When I checked earlier they were all right."

I thought about walking him up to the 10th floor so he could get a look at the flooded city with fires burning and all that stuff, but I figured I'd spare him. We went to the break room instead. It was packed with people playing cards, dominoes, and eating lunch. "Come over here and look out this window — can you see your car?" I asked my dad as I pointed in the direction of our cars.

"Damn. That water is pretty high. Is that my car over there?" he asked.

Pointing to the left I said, "One to the left in the back corner.

See mine, the blue one?"

After a pause he said, "Oh yeah, it's okay. We'll be all right." Incredulous, I said, "It's halfway up over your tires. See?"

"I can't see that far, Son. If it floods, it floods. What the hell?"

"I guess it depends on where the water flows. We'll have to wait and see."

Deciding to change the subject I asked him if he was hungry yet.

Looking at me somewhat apologetically, he said, "I could eat something, I guess."

Walking down the middle corridor, my dad stopped in front of the huge fan to cool off for a minute. It was nearing noontime, and the heat was stifling. Absolutely stifling. I worried about him. Once we got to "our area" I took my food bag and dumped it onto his mattress so he could pick something out to eat. He said he'd forgotten to go to the store (which I figured). I had a little extra food for both of us just in case. "I've got a couple cans of Hormel tamales here, two cans of soup, a can of raviolis, some pork and beans."

After touching everything I put on the mattress, he finally grabbed a can and said, "I'll eat so me tamales. They're not the spicy kind, are they? I can't eat anything too spicy."

"Nope. They're the regular kind. I'm going to put them in this Tupperware dish right here and go warm them up for you in the microwave."

Before I could finish, he said, "I need something to drink."

"I've got some lemonade or ice tea packs you can mix in a bottle of water."

"I'll take a tea. You got ice?"

"Yeah right dad! Look in that blue bag right there and grab a bottle of water."

I tried to fit as much water in my bag as I could, just in case. I brought two duffel bags and one small cooler bag filled with granola bars, drink packs, and canned food. Lora had insisted on it.

My two duffel bags had clothes, water, and my portable DVD player with movies in it. Picking up the can of tamales and the can opener, I told my dad, "I'll be right back."

When I got to the break room, I saw that the microwave was gone. I asked one of the deputies where it was and he said, "They came and got it because it wasn't working."

I hastily replied, "I saw someone using it at breakfast." The deputy just shrugged his shoulders and left the break room. I went back by dad and told him the microwave was broken.

Not looking fazed, he said, "That's all right, son, I'll just eat 'em cold. I eat stuff cold a lot. It's not a big deal."

"You sure? I can try and find you a sandwich or something." At that point, he reached up and took the dish right out of my hand, almost spilling it on him. He peeled the paper covering off each of the tamales, eating them with his fingers.

I was a little surprised by this and said, "Hold on a minute. I have a fork in my bag — here!" With his mouth half full and red juice on his finger and thumb, he took the fork and continued eating. I chuckled a little to myself.

When he was finished he had one left and proceeded to wrap it in some sort of paper and save it for later. Old people with their "save anything" mentality! When he did this, it reminded me of a day about a year or so earlier when I was eating lunch at the golf course. My friend and I had just finished playing golf and had started to eat lunch when my dad walked into the clubhouse and sat down with us. Corey had just finished eating a burger and had about 10 French fries left on his plate. Without even asking, my dad reached over and took a couple of fries off of his plate and proceeded to eat them. As he was chewing them he said to Corey, "You finished with those fries?"

With a big grin, Corey said, "I guess I am now! Why you want the rest?"

"Yeah, I think I'll take them home and eat them later."

Corey and I couldn't believe our eyes when my dad took to a napkin and put the few fries in it, roll it up and put it in his pocket. Here's a guy who could go eat anywhere or better yet, order some food, but he decides to take a few French fries home for later.

I tell you, old folks can really make you laugh. I guess his thriftiness was left over from surviving the Great Depression.

"You gonna eat that tamale later?"

"Oh, yeah, Son. Never waste food!"

Jokingly, I told him, "Save me a piece for later, all right?"

He looked at me a little funny, "You want a piece later?"

"I'm just kidding with you, Pops — it's all yours." After that little bit of entertainment, I went back over by T.C. and the radio. "Any other news?"

"You shoulda' heard what they were saying about the Superdome! They said some of the people over there are committing suicide; people are gettin' raped, killed! Complete chaos!"

"What? You're kidding!" I was stunned.

"They also said that part of the roof blew off the 'dome as well."

I was starting to get a bad mental picture of what the city looked like. It was falling apart, and there was no help on the way that I knew of.

I said another silent prayer.

For the next couple of hours, I sat on the floor by T.C. and his wife, listening to the radio. We talked about different things as we heard the unfolding, unending, shocking news.

Periodically, I checked on my dad. He was either reading the three-day-old newspaper or going over by the smoking area. I was starting to notice he was smoking a little more than usual. He didn't appear nervous, but I'm sure he was.

Chapter Five

I T WAS APPROACHING 2:30 P. M. ON TUESDAY, AUGUST 30TH and I had to start getting ready for work. Word was starting to spread they were going to begin evacuating the inmates first. There was 100 percent confirmation on the levee breaks, and the 17th Street Canal levee break was on the Orleans Parish side, filling the city with floodwaters from the lake. We were only about six to seven miles from the breach, and the water outside was steadily rising. I ran over to the break room to look at our cars. The water was up to the door on my dad's car and halfway up the wheel of my car. I still had hope the waters would recede and we could get out of there, although my dad's car wasn't looking good.

Walking back to get dressed for work, I overheard a ranking official tell a deputy, "They only have enough food left to feed the inmates one meal a day for another day or two, max." I would soon find out the warehouse and the main kitchen for the entire facility were completely flooded and unusable.

Making my way up the stairs, I saw a door open to what I thought was a maintenance area. This area was between the second and third floors of the building. This was the first time I'd been in that area and my curiosity was piqued when I heard some voices.

One of them sounded like my supervisor's, Nurse Robert. He's the nurse supervisor for the Psychiatric Department and is a commissioned deputy for the sheriff's office.

I crept into the dark, stinky area.

This building has had about 75 years of hard use and it looked like it. Upon entering, there are some metal stairs that go down about six feet to the floor. A few huge steel tanks stand to the right, with a wall directly to the left. About 20 feet past that, the area opens up slightly. To the left, ahead about 30 feet, there are some double doors leading to an area I never knew existed. Robert and a couple of deputies were there.

"Hey Robert, I was on my way up to the 10th floor, and I thought I heard your voice. What is this place?"

In a matter-of-fact tone he replied, "In short, this is the main plumbing and waste management area. Pretty nasty, huh?" As soon as he said that, a little rat scurried down a ledge and into a hole in the wall.

Pointing behind him, I said, "What's behind those doors?" "That's the outside of the building. Come check it out."

We had to step up on a wooden crate and when the doors swung open, we were standing outside on top of the second floor roof of the House of Detention, directly above the cafeteria area. It took me a moment to realize we were on a flat roof area. A huge extension expanded out around the entire building in the shape of an upside down letter "T". The inmates' recreational area was to the right of the center part and barbed wire went all around the perimeter. The area was filled with three or four feet of water, making it look like a big cesspool.

We walked around the south portion and I could see the water level and my car pretty well. My dad's car definitely had water in it now and the water level was up to the bottom of my door. It looked like it was just a matter of time now before they both were swamped.

"Son of a bitch!" I exclaimed.

Robert turned to me, "What's wrong, Gavin?"

"My dad's car is about gone and mine's next. Look, my car is the only one in the lot that doesn't have water in it yet!"

"Yeah, you might as well kiss that baby goodbye. Too bad. It looks pretty new."

"Yeah, I've only had it a little over a year ... damn!"

We examined the damage around the entire building. Hundreds of cars littered the streets. Even if my car miraculously survived, we weren't going to be able to drive out of there. It was clear things had worsened. We were in crisis mode.

Wiping the sweat from my face, I took one last look at my car, then the brilliant sky and a few fires burning in the distance.

I told Nurse Robert I was going upstairs and went back through the doors. When I closed the doors it was nearly pitch black. I could see the faintest light shining around the wall by the metal stairs. I had visions of rats dropping on me and gnawing on my head or something. I quickly navigated to the metal stairs and out of the area.

The stairwell from there to the 10th floor was extremely hot. Even the walls were "sweating." The eighth and ninth floor inmates chanted and rattled the bars loudly. Those floors held disciplinary and some high profile inmates. Those individuals tend to manipulate the system and always try to get their way. When they're caught in their little games, they are sent to the "hole" as punishment with no television or "store" [commissary] privileges. The hole is where inmates go who get out of line, fight or get caught doing something they're not supposed to. The best way to describe it would be like sending your kid to his or her room for punishment, but in this case they would be in the room the size of a closet with bars instead of a door.

The 10th floor was pretty quiet when I got there, which was quite different from the day before. Nurses Cecilia and Urban were putting medical charts in garbage bags.

"Whatcha' doin'?" I asked.

Hurried, Cecilia said, "Robert just sent word and said to get all the charts together and the medications because they will be moving the inmates soon."

I just saw Robert and he didn't say anything. "Where are they sending them?"

"Either Hunts or Angola." Angola is the Louisiana State Penitentiary — one of the roughest prisons in the country.

"When?" I asked.

"Soon. Grab a bag and give us a hand," Cecilia said.

After about 10 minutes, I remembered the inmates up there needed their medications. "What about med pass?" I asked.

Both Cecilia and Urban recalled their duties.

"Damn. Gavin, why don't you start packing while Urban and I finish this?" Cecilia said.

"Did anybody count the narcotics yet?" I asked.

Urban handed me the lock box key and said, "Why don't you do it real quick, if you feel the need."

"Hey y'all, I'm gonna go find Robert and see if I can pack a few days worth of meds so we don't have to do it every shift, especially if they get moved."

Nurse Urban pointed out that a lot of the psychiatric meds couldn't be in the heat for too long. "Don't pack any Depakote (for bipolar disorder) or any gel cap pills. Can y'all think of any others?"

"I'll grab the drug book and look up as many as I can."

Great. Just when I thought I might have an easy night was slammed right off the bat.

I ran down the stairs to try and catch Robert by the mezzanine. He wasn't there, so I went to the second floor to see if anyone had seen him. Nurse Yolanda said she thought he was in his father -in-law's office. Robert's father-in-law, a no-nonsense guy, is in charge of the building. After my knock on the door, I heard a strong New Orleans-accented voice say, "Who's that?"

After announcing myself, I was told to come in.

"Yes, sir. I'm looking for Robert. Have you seen him?"

He boomed back, "Robert, come here." After about 15 seconds, Robert opened the door while wiping his face with a towel.

"Hey Gav, what's up?"

"We're up on 10 packing meds and getting the charts together. Is it all right if we get a few days' of meds just in case the inmates get moved by morning?"

Robert looked at his father-in-law and then at me and shrugged his shoulder saying, "Y'all do whatever you want — at this point I don't really care."

"All right. Will do." And with that, I hiked back up the sweltering stairwell to the 10th floor.

When I got there, I looked out over the city for a minute. We were surrounded by water for as far as I could see, but I couldn't tell where it was pouring in from. Parts of the 17th Street Canal could be seen from my building, but I couldn't see where the break in the levee was. One of the St. Bernard deputies had a radio and was sitting in the file room right across from the medical office.

"You mind turning that radio up?" someone asked.

Almost simultaneously I also heard, "Hey Gavin, what did Robert say?"

"We can do whatever we want. He doesn't care," I replied. I found about three or four medications we use that are sensitive to heat and alerted the other two nurses. When they finished what they were doing, we packed the meds for about an hour and a half, adjusting for the heat-sensitive meds. During this time, I asked Urban about J.W.

"What's up with our little Elvis — J.W. Is he alive?"

"I think they just tried to bring him by boat, but Charity wasn't accepting anybody — they're under water as well."

"What? Where is he now?" I asked.

"I think Dr. Marcus was monitoring him. I'm not sure. They think he was bottoming out (dangerously low blood pressure) from taking too much Thorazine." Thorazine is an older anti-psychotic medication that can cause dangerously low blood pressures when taken in excess.

J.W. is so disturbed he was on a pretty high dose. Coupled with the fact he fell and cut his head, he was probably going to have this problem eventually. Of course, it had to happen in the middle of this disastrous hurricane with no way to get him to the hospital.

"I hope you're right, Urban. I really don't want to deal with that situation. I have to keep an eye on my dad."

Nurse Urban asked, "Hey Gavin, how old is your dad anyways?"

"Eighty three years young; but if you ask him he will bet you that you can't guess his age."

"Why do say that?"

Laughing a little I replied, "Something to do with magic Sun-Chlorella tablets, his fountain of youth. When you see him ask him how old he is. You'll get a laugh."

We all sat around for a little while listening to the radio. The news was getting worse and worse. The gloominess in the radio announcer's voice became strangely hypnotic: "There are reports of devastation all over the city... gas lines are starting to rupture, causing numerous fires. The water is continuing to pour into the city... downtown New Orleans looks like a nuclear bomb went off... shards of glass everywhere downtown... the Central Business District is covered with glass and debris. Many of the hotel windows downtown are blown out... drapes and sheets just hanging out of the windows... dead bodies floating in flood waters! We have reports of people calling 911 and our radio station for help from their attics..."

Cecilia cut in, "This is horrible! I can't imagine being stuck in an attic during the storm. And in this heat!" After a few seconds of silence, she got up. "I'm going to pass out these meds. I can't listen to this anymore." Urban and I looked at each other, nodded our heads in unison, and got up to pass out medications.

On the med pass some inmates asked us what was going on. A couple of them said they could hear the radio, but couldn't understand what was being said. The television didn't work and you could see nervousness on their faces.

"What's going on?"

"Why we only got one sandwich today?"

"We need water too. We haven't gotten any water today. Water, please!"

"What's going to happen to us?"

Prisoners of Katrina

I decided to get everyone's attention. "Listen up guys! We're surrounded by water. Some of the levees have collapsed and water is pouring into the city."

Interrupting me at times, inmates yelled out things like, "I'm supposed to roll-out tomorrow (roll-out means get released)," or "I need to call my people."

"Hold up guys, hear me out. The phones don't work, and there is nowhere to roll out to. You'll be evacuated soon. I don't know when. We're low on food and water..."

They all started yelling and chattering and asking all kinds of questions I couldn't answer. I finished passing meds on the tier, and then I had to go down to the seventh floor, since that's where we keep some of the chronic psychiatric inmates.

Those people are schizophrenics, bi-polars, psychotics, or otherwise seriously mentally ill. Some are homeless and others have families but have been disowned. It's pretty sad to see, and I try to do what I can for them. Most of them are arrested for penny-ante stuff like obstruction of a public sidewalk, trespassing, sleeping in a public park, drunk in public, and things of that nature. The laws in New Orleans are capriciously enforced, and those people are easy targets. At least 90 percent of them are African-American and many have a history of alcohol or drug abuse. It is a common occurrence that in the city, if you're a black male and look a certain way, you have a good chance of getting arrested numerous times. It's sad.

I went down to the seventh floor, and it was hot as Hell there.

Many of those guys were lying in all kinds of positions on their mattresses on the floor. Family members, staff, and friends. Since we were running on generators, the fans weren't operating. The heat was stifling, and I could see the exhaustion on their faces. There were only two toilets everyone had to share, and there was one grimy, antiquated shower at the beginning of the tier for everyone to use. The newer part of the facility across the street had air conditioning and a modernized set-up. The main administrative building also housed federal and illegal alien inmates. The building has many floors and is as tall as the HOD building I was in.

One of the regular inmates on the seventh floor, K.R., saw me coming down the tier. "Hey nurse, hey nurse... you got my meds?"

"Hang on K, I'll get them to you in a minute." After walking the length of the tier and getting everyone's attention, I told them the same thing I told the inmates on the 10th floor. The reaction was similar and so were the questions. Ignoring most, I passed the medications out, explaining to them why certain meds were not given. I'm not really sure if they understood or not, but I tried to give them the courtesy of telling them why I was doing what I was doing.

After finishing the medication pass, I went back to the 10th floor. Cecelia was gone, and Urban and I each grabbed a mop and mopped the medical office and the surrounding walkways, in case we had any emergencies.

Normally, Urban works the "graveyard" shift from 11 p.m. to 7:30 a.m. He is a very interesting character. I don't think I can describe him very well, but he's a very knowledgeable person and an outstanding nurse. He was helping us out on this shift, which I greatly appreciated. Once we finished cleaning up (we never really finished — too much water) we started talking about his family and mine. He wasn't sure if his father evacuated or not. He brought his mother to the facility with him and she was a godsend.

She is a diminutive Latino lady who appears to have Bell's palsy or something, since the left side of her face droops. She's extremely feisty and has a very strong Central American accent. At times, she was hard to understand.

After we talked for an hour or so, Urban went back downstairs and I asked him to keep an eye on my dad. I don't know why I was extra worried about my father, but I was.

Around that time, Nurse Favis came to the 10th floor. We usually work together on the evening shift. She apologized for coming up late, saying she had lost track of time. She had her daughter with her, and she was trying to entertain her and keep an eye on her. I told her not too worry about her tardiness, and for the next couple hours it was relatively quiet. We had only one fistfight and no one was hurt badly. I gave her an update of what we did with the medical charts and the medication pass.

The highlight of being on the 10th floor was J.W.'s return. I don't really know what happened, but the doctors sent him back, and we were to check his vital signs every hour for the next 48 hours or as long as he was here. They must have stabilized him long enough to feel he was all right. When he saw me, he greeted me with his usual, "Hey, Dad!" It never gets old to me. I always laugh a little on the inside. We're basically the same age and it's funny he keeps calling me "Dad." Sometimes I try to imagine how it must be to be out of touch with reality. With the situation at hand, ignorance would've truly been bliss.

We decided to shuffle some of the inmates around and keep J.W. in a cell by the front of the north tier by himself. I wasn't completely comfortable he was out of the woods, health-wise. We thought if we kept him by himself maybe he would stay calm. We told him not to play in the dirty water on the floor, and if he did we would place him in five-point restraints, which are used for inmates who are acting bizarre, hostile, or suicidal. This is the best method I have seen to control an inmate. It is amazing how fast they change their minds about being suicidal or violent. It doesn't always work, but usually it does. Restraints are used because every inmate cannot be watched at all times. If something happens to that inmate or another inmate, the sheriff's office is ultimately responsible.

We got J.W. settled in, and I notified the deputy that a couple of the tiers were low on drinking water. The deputy said he knew and had notified the Watch Office. "They're just gonna have to wait. Nothing I can do about it right now." When the inmates were told this, they complained loudly.

It was just about dark outside as the sun slipped under the orange-blue skyline. Plumes of smoke blended with the darkening horizon. Not a single streetlight could be seen in the distance. Taking one last look at our cars, I could see the roof of my dad's car and I couldn't really tell, but it looked like the water was about midway up my door. Every car in the lot was flooded. They looked like matchbox cars in a large muddy puddle. Favis came over and pointed out her car. All I could see was the back section of the roof.

"I'm so glad that piece of junk got flooded. Now I can get somethin' else. Always givin' me trouble."

I interjected, "Not me — my car is only a year old. I'm sure I'm gonna get screwed on my insurance."

It was strangely calm and quiet. We only had light down the hallways of the 10th floor and the tiers. The two bathrooms on the 10th floor for the medical staff and security to use weren't working. As you might imagine, the toilet was not pleasant, and that's putting it mildly.

I hate to say it, but I urinated in the sink.

The circumstances made us all do things we wouldn't have normally done.

It seemed like every time I sat down to listen to the radio, the announcers sounded just flat-out deflated. After 20 or so minutes of listening to it, I asked Favis if I could go down a little early and check on my dad. She pleasantly replied, "Sure, I've got it up here." It was amazing to see how my coworkers kept their calm and pulled together as the situation worsened.

"Come get me if you need something; and don't forget to

check on J.W. See ya later," I said.

I felt a lot better physically that day than the day before. I only had to go up and down the stairs a few times. It was still inferno-hot and completely dark in the stairwell. Passing up the mezzanine I heard some voices, but decided to keep on moving.

I made my way through the doorway and onto the second floor. A few stragglers walked around, but most people were sleeping or listening to the radio. Some talked about the other buildings in the facility that had lost power completely and were under four to eight feet of water. Some inmates were trying to escape, but none were successful, as far as we knew.

I saw Dr. Marcus; he told me that IPC and Templeman buildings I, II, III, and IV were completely swamped with water.

"I was sleeping on a couch in TP I and II last night and when I woke up and sat up my legs were in water. We had to move to the third floor and then all you could hear was the rattle of bars and hateful chorus of the inmates, "Kill the white mother fuckers! Kill the white mother fuckers! Kill the …" Dr. Marcus had valiantly moved from building to building in the water by swimming or floating on something. By Tuesday afternoon, he had pretty much settled at our building, House of Detention.

I overheard all kinds of stuff while I was changing my shirt over by my mattress. My dad was sleeping, and I thought I wouldn't disturb him. It was around 10 p.m., and I decided to clean up a little. I had a couple gallons of Kentwood Spring Water so I took my towel, poured some water on it and wiped my face, neck, arms, and armpits.

After putting some deodorant on, I grabbed my toothbrush and toothpaste and went to the bathroom sink near us. I tried to turn on one of the faucets, figuring that it wouldn't work, and it didn't. I poured some bottled water into a cup, put some toothpaste on my toothbrush, and brushed away. It was about this time that I noticed the bathroom stunk really, really badly. The overuse was starting to show. There was a trash all over the floor, and I could tell there wasn't any concern to keep the bathroom somewhat clean.

I made the decision at that point that I wasn't going to eat until I was absolutely starving so I could avoid going to the bathroom as much as possible. It dawned on me trying to convince my dad to do the same would be a difficult task.

I settled in to my mattress and put on my portable DVD player and started to watch the movie, "Left Behind," a movie about the End Times with references to the Bible's Book of Revelations.

How appropriate.

I had been watching the movie for only a little while when the whole building went completely dark. A few kids and others screamed, some laughed, and gradually a few flashlights flickered on.

About five minutes later, the ranking official in charge of the building walked in and with his booming voice announced, "Everybody listen up! The generator is flooded, and we are out of power!"

As he talked, two deputies walked in with crowbars and shotguns. They ordered everyone who was near a window (that was us) to move their things so they could break the windows to try and get some air to circulate. I woke my dad and helped him sit up.

Sounding completely confused and startled he asked, "What the hell is going on? Why is it so dark in here?"

"The power is out, Dad. The generator is flooded," I explained. "Get up. Hurry up! We've got to move our stuff away from the window so they can bust them out."

"Do what?" He was confused.

"Just get up and stand over there."

While we moved our things, I could hear the boss saying, "Everybody stay calm. We're making arrangements to evacuate everyone. For safety reasons, we'll be moving the inmates first." I could hear people starting to complain, but it made sense to me to move the inmates first. "Everyone will be evacuated! Please be patient! That's it!"

The deputies started to smash the thick windows with the crowbars as the boss walked away, the shattered glass falling in small pieces to the floor. The window to my left started to crack open, and the other deputy struck another window. Further away, Corporal Mitchell came up and stood next to me, but I didn't really pay much attention to him.

Then, **BANG!** I heard a gun go off and a sharp pain hit my right leg. My heart felt like it was in my stomach.

The deputy jumped and almost dropped the crowbar on his head. It was so dark in there that no one but the deputy, Corporal Mitchell, and I knew that the gun wasn't aimed at the window. After looking at the deputy, I grabbed the candle off of the nearby table and shined it in the direction of my leg and saw that it was bleeding. I looked over to my right and could see a horrified look on Corporal Mitchell's face.

I cried out, "What the fuck happened?!"

"The gun accidentally went off in my hand. Holy Shit! I almost shot my foot off, man."

"You almost shot your foot? You almost shot my fucking leg off man! You trying to kill me or what?"

Half whispering he said, "Shhhhhh! Man ... it was an accident. I thought the safety was on. This mutha' fucker has a hair trigger on it!" Simultaneously, we both looked at the floor with his flashlight and we could see where the shot put a black mark a couple of inches wide. The piece of the floor must have hit my leg.

"You got my heart racing!"

"Mine too. Damn! That was close." I grabbed a towel from out of my bag and wiped my leg while Corporal Mitchell explained to me this shotgun was actually an air gun used for impact and did not use bullets or shells.

Thank God for that or I might be a one-legged nurse! It took about five minutes of whacking the window to get most of the glass out. It was after 11 p.m., and the second floor was alive and kicking.

You could hear frantic conversations and tension in people's voices. We got some brooms and dustpans so we could clean up the glass on the floor. Using a couple of flashlights and a candle, we picked up the bigger chunks by hand, trying not to cut ourselves in the process.

Once the area was swept up, we started to put our stuff back in its spot. Deputy Jeanne and her boyfriend had a couple candles lit on the table we had moved back by the wall. One had an image of what appeared to be a Spanish-looking Jesus Christ on it. It was made of glass and about a foot tall. It lit up the area quite well, considering how dark it was.

I got my dad's mattress situated against the wall again and put the sheet back on it for him. I turned to tell him to lie back down but he wasn't there. T.C. was over by his spot. I asked him where my dad was and he said he saw him walking towards the visitors' area. I went over there to find him sitting at the end of the walkway smoking a cigarette. "Hey, your bed is made and your stuff is back where it was, okay? You all right?"

Shining the flashlight in his direction, I could see he was a little concerned, but he would never admit it to me. "Oh, yeah, Son. I'll be over there in a minute."

It was also apparent he wanted to be alone so I said, "I'm gong back over to fix my bed. See you in a minute." Walking away, I looked back and noticed he was lighting up another cigarette. This confirmed he was becoming increasingly uneasy with the situation — just like the rest of us.

Back by our spot, I put a sheet on my mattress and Deputy Kite asked, "Is your daddy all right?"

"I guess so. I just think he's out of his element, and he doesn't quite know what to think of all this. I'm a little worried about him."

"If there is anything I can do just let me know."

"I appreciate that. Thanks."

For the next few minutes, I sat quietly and listened to everything going on around me. My mind was starting to race. My dad came back and gingerly laid down next to me on his mattress. "Everything all right, Pops?"

"Think we'll be going home soon?"

"I'm not sure, but I hope so."

"I do too because I need my medicine soon. I'm gonna try and get some sleep."

Damn. I had forgotten he was running low on his medication. Coupled with his increased smoking, I worried about his health. I didn't want anything to happen to him. He deserved better; we all did. With all the horrible things I was hearing on the radio, I was glad he was with me, but not in the jail with me.

"Good night, Dad."

"Good night, Son."

I fixed a stare at the candle on the table. The Jesus image on the candle looked right at me. I have never been ultra-religious or anything, but just looking at that lit image had a calming effect. Everyone around us started to settle down a little bit. The bathroom was only about 30 feet from our mattresses, and people were going in and out at a steady pace. In the night, there was one problem: the bathroom had only a sliding latch on it and no doorstopper. When someone would go in, they would close the door, slamming it loudly. It was annoying at night to be asleep and then abruptly awakened with the slamming door. Some people were considerate and closed the door slowly, except the younger teenagers. It was like they were trying to make the loudest noise by having the door slam behind them.

Chapter Six

WE' D BEEN TRAPPED FOR ALMOST FOUR DAYS. It was after midnight, and my dad had fallen asleep, which made me feel a little better. For as late as it was, it was extremely hot and muggy, like sauna hot. A hint of a warm breeze would come through the jagged window from time to time, but it didn't do much good.

When I laid my head down on the pillow, I could see outside to the sky through a small part of the window. Words can't describe how I felt. The stars in the sky were truly amazing — billions and billions of bright stars. With all the lights out, you could see the night sky in unbelievable detail. Chills went down my entire body. I have been out in the countryside before and have never seen that many stars at night.

I was drawn to it. I got up off my mattress and carefully stuck my head out of the narrow, glass-splintered window. There were still some glass pieces sticking out of the window and I really didn't feel like getting one of my ears cut off. It was phenomenal though, like the Milky Way was blanketing New Orleans: clear, crisp and sparkling.

I felt the power of the universe upon us.

For what we were going through, all those stars shining made me believe there was a higher power looking over us.

With the devastation surrounding us, the beautiful midnight sky was truly something to behold.

I will never forget the feeling of peace and awe and wonder I had at that moment.

Then suddenly, **pop, pop, POW... Pop, POW POW!** Gunshots pierced the serene silence.

Stunned, I quickly but carefully pulled my head back in through the jagged window. That was the first time in my life I had ever heard live gunfire close by like that. And it didn't stop there. It seemed like every 15 minutes or so, for the next couple of hours, I heard a gunshot here, two or three there.

Bang, bang POW POW! Pop POW POW POW!

I didn't know if they were coming from the police, deputies, civilians, or what. This was all starting to feel like a bad movie. I was afraid for my dad and myself.

We obviously were in survival mode. Lying there I looked out the shattered window, my mind racing. I couldn't fall asleep with all that was going on. I wasn't sure, but it felt like my air mattress was starting to sink just as our hopes were. I grabbed the flashlight and looked under and around the mattress and checked the air hole, but didn't see anything wrong.

If I had to guess, it was after two o'clock in the morning by then, and I hadn't gotten any sleep. Lying back down, I took a few deep breaths to try to help me go to sleep.

It must have worked but before I knew it, **"KABOOM!"** A

huge explosion went off that scared me right off my half-deflated mattress.

What the hell was that?

It was still dark so I reached for my cell phone and turned it on to see what the time was. For as loud as that was, I was grateful my dad stayed asleep. It was 5:12 a.m., and my phone still had no signal. It was still dark and the stars were still brilliantly twinkling through the broken window.

It was Heaven and Hell all at once.

I had to go to the bathroom, so I turned my flashlight on and navigated my way there. After carefully closing the door, an eye-popping stench smacked me in the face. Now the plumbing didn't work.

I put the flashlight under my left armpit and pulled my shirt up over my nose and took a pee. Then I went back to my bed and attempted to get some sleep. As soon as I lay down, my dad woke up and told me he had to go to the bathroom, so I told him I would go with him. I planned to show him how bad it was and maybe he could wait.

"I got it, Son."

Whispering, I asked him, "Number one or number two?"

"What?"

"Come on, it's dark and I'll help you with the flashlight. Come on." Looking around real quick, I grabbed the sheet off of my bed and brought it with us.

"What's that for?" he asked.

"I'll let you know in a minute."

After almost tripping over a couple of people we made it to the bathroom. Once inside I shined the flashlight on the toilets so he could see the piles of human waste.

"Goddamn. I'm not going in there!"

"Look, Dad, I'm gonna tear this sheet and cover the sink. You can sit on top and go in there. It's better than the alternative."

"I guess so, Son." The sheet was worn anyway, and I didn't want to risk either one of us getting sick from the heaps of urine - soaked feces in the bathroom. I tore a piece just big enough to cover the sink. After helping him up on the sink, I walked to the back on the side of the bathroom and grabbed a roll of toilet paper for him. I walked over by the door so he could do his business.

There was a shattered window in the bathroom, and after he was done I took the sheet, tied it up and threw it out the window into the water, which was at least ten feet high. We both looked at each other and broke out into laughter.

What else could we do?

I told him to wait a second and I would be right back. I went back to our spot, grabbed my towel and a bottle of water, and brought it back to the bathroom. I told him to hold his hands out and cup them and I poured the water in his hands, and then used the towel to dry his hands. Once we were done, we walked back, by flashlight, to our area.

It was after 6 a.m. by now and some sunlight was just beginning to creep through the broken window by our spot. It was extremely hot for that time of the day, and I knew it was going to be a very long, hot, humid one. I told my dad I was not going to eat much so I could avoid the bathroom as much as I possible, hoping he'd take the hint. I took a couple sips of water and encouraged him to do the same. He did and lay back down. I told him I had a few pairs of shorts with me if he wanted a pair to wear.

"You got something to fit me?"

"Not really, but you can leave the top button open and I think that might work." I had a baggy pair with a drawstring at the top that he could probably fit into.

"Here you go, Pops." He sat back and took his pants off. Thank God he had boxer briefs on and it was still early in the morning. He put the shorts on saying, "Ah ... that's better. You wear these, Son?" They were plaid shorts that could be used for swimming.

Jokingly, I replied, "You never know, we might have to swim out of here."

He turned to me real quick and said, "What?"

"I'm kidding, Dad. I'll be right back. I'm going to look out the window to see how our cars are doing."

While I was on the way to the break room, I noticed there were a lot more people sleeping in the big hallway than the night before. It was dark and I needed my flashlight to maneuver through it. I wondered about the batteries. As you might expect, our cars were surrounded by a watery grave. What little hope I had held out was crushed in the bright morning sun. The water was now three-quarters of the way up my window and obviously over the hood of the car. Cars that I could see the day before were no longer visible. The water was a dark brownish color and had what looked like oil slicks covering most of it.

I was really numb at this point, wondering how Lora was doing and realizing now I didn't have a car and neither did my dad. We're both very independent people, but it was clear we would be joined at the hip for a while. A minute or two later, I heard what sounded like the engine of a flat boat. After watching the boat go around the building, I went back by my dad and told him the bad news. "Well, Dad, you want the bad news or the bad news?"

"What?"

"You can barely see the roof of your car and the water is three-quarters of the way up the window of my car."

"Well, when the water goes down, maybe she'll start up!"

"Your car is completely submerged in the water. She ain't startin'." I could see he didn't want to accept this and sat there absorbing it in silence.

Suddenly, he asked, "When are we going home?" I paused before answering because I could feel myself starting to get frustrated and angry. I could see he didn't really comprehend the severity of the situation. I had to give it to him straight.

"Dad, listen, we don't know how your place is. I don't know how my place is. We need to get the hell out of here first and foremost. Forget about going home any time soon. Let's try and get out of here first."

"But the storm is over. When the water goes down we'll just catch a ride."

At this point, I could see he really believed this would be over soon. I tried to explain, "The levees have collapsed, Dad. There's water pouring into the city from the lake, maybe the river... I don't know. The water isn't going down any time soon. I'll try to find what's going on in the next couple of hours. I'll let you know when I find something out."

The smell of diesel gas had filled the room. I decided to go investigate. It was after 7 a.m., and no one was in the Watch Office. I heard someone say all the deputies and ranking officials were having a meeting. I thought I would run up to the 10th floor to take a look at the city.

There were only a few people up there. Nurse Donna was just finishing up her shift. "What's up Gavin? Why are you up here so early?"

"I came up to take a look at the city. How was last night?"

"Not too bad. Typical stuff."

I went over to the south side to look out the window. The sky was cloudless: beautiful, clear, and hopeful. It was strange that since the hurricane passed through we hadn't had a cloud in the sky.

It was as if we were starting over. But there wasn't any breeze at all, either.

I saw a couple military helicopters in the distance. When I went to the north side, I saw a massive plume of black smoke flowing from the east, like ink flowing up into the placid heavens.

"Jesus! Did y'all see that smoke over there?" Before they could answer, I said, "I heard a huge explosion this morning around five o'clock. That must be where the smoke is coming from."

Nobody really acknowledged me. It was as if we were helplessly watching Rome burn. "Hey Donna, did you see that smoke out there?"

"What smoke? Where?"

"Come see. Over there."

"Damn! Where the hell is that coming from?"

"I have no idea, but I heard an explosion a couple of hours ago so I guess that's where it's coming from. This is turning into Baghdad west."

After about 10 minutes of looking at the worsening situation, I went back downstairs to see if I could find out where that diesel smell was coming from. When I got to the second floor, there were more people walking around. I saw Nurse Favis and asked her.

"You smell that?" I asked.

"Yeah, smells like diesel gas or something," she said, with a funny look on her face.

In unison, we asked, *Where's that coming from?*

Laughing as I walked away, I said, "When I find out I'll let you know."

"All right, G."

I finally found Nurse Robert and asked him about the smell. He said, "I was told that the flood water overflowed the generator and went down the exhaust pipes and that's where it's coming from."

"Sounds right to me. Thanks. Hey, are you going up to the 10th floor today?"

"Nope. I'm pretty much a deputy from here on out."

"By the way, when are we getting out of here?" I asked.

"Hopefully soon."

Unfortunately, that would be a recurring theme. I went back over to see my dad. "Hey, Dad. That smell is coming ..." It didn't look like he understood me too well so I didn't want to confuse him anymore. "Don't worry about it, Dad. Just hang in there. They're working on getting us out of here."

"Okay, Son. I'm a little hungry."

Grabbing my bag, I took some granola bars out to show him. "I have peanut butter, oatmeal raisin, chocolate chip ..."

"Chocolate chip!"

"Here you go. Do you want some water or lemonade?" I asked.

"A cup of coffee would be great."

"We don't have any power to make any coffee, Pops. Here — drink a few sips of water."

It was approaching 8 a.m. and the heat was already starting to be a factor. The bathroom odor had made its way around the second floor. We were only 10 yards or so from the bathroom, and it seemed like every other person was letting the door slam. My dad said, "I'll be right back," and started to walk toward the visitors' area, I assumed to catch a smoke. A few kids ran around making noise as other people sat around listening to the radio or talking among themselves.

I saw T.C. and his wife adjusting the antenna on their radio, so I made my way over to them. "What's up T.C.?"

"Hey G, whatcha' say?"

About that time the radio announcer was saying something about looters. "We have people running around looting downtown New Orleans. We have reports of an NOPD officer being shot in the back of the head by a looter. He's in critical condition at West Jefferson Medical Center ... the suspect is also there with injuries as well."

T.C. and I exchanged wide-eyed looks and just shook our heads. "Man, this is crazy, Gavin."

Two days after the storm and cops were being shot!

"Pretty unbelievable. I wonder what the hell is next?"

We turned our attention back to the radio as the announcer continued, "There are areas of the city where the water looks like it's boiling. The gas lines are rupturing and igniting numerous fires around the metro area ... the fire department is stretched so thin they're letting some of the fires just burn. The water pressure is almost non-existent ... no part of the city is exempt from the fires. We have families just standing on corners looking dazed ... thousands upon thousands of people with no food or water ... BODIES floating in the water near the Superdome ... chaos at the New Orleans Convention Center with reports of gun battles, fighting, rapes ..." and so on.

A horrid picture.

Where was our mayor? Our governor? Our president? Was help coming?

I sat there wondering what was going to happen to us. The situation was dire. The inmates were riotously loud and it was getting hotter by the minute.

I got up and told T.C., "I'll be back in a little while." Walking back over to my spot, I felt tears welling up in my eyes.

I couldn't help it. I don't know why, I just had this sudden feeling of complete helplessness. My emotions were childlike.

Images flashed through my mind like a high-speed movie. I remembered, as a kid, my dad being so much older, and I would worry he would die or not be there for some reason or the other. After my parents divorced when I was eight, it took me a long time to get past this fear. My mother eventually remarried, and I have to say my dad was there for me every step of the way. Now here we were in this nightmare.

So this is what it's come to?

What did we do to deserve this?

Would he expire here?

Was this it?

Here's a man who was born in the 1920s, grew up in the Great Depression, made it through World War II, and was a fairly well-known jazz musician in the city. He'd played with greats like Louie Prima and Al Hirt. He had started a long career at the world-famous Roosevelt Hotel in New Orleans and then the Blue Room in the Fairmont Hotel for over 35 years, and had even been on the Tonight Show with Harry Connick Jr.

After 83 years of a pretty good life, he was in one of the worst situations ever.

It's hard for me to convey exactly what was going on in my head. The bottom line was my dad is a good man and had been very good to me, and I just didn't want anything to happen to him. Those feelings poured out like a volcano erupting. It was then I steeled my resolve to do whatever it took to keep him safe and his mind right. I knew this would be one of the greatest challenges of my life. I had to figure out a way to get him to understand what we were facing without upsetting or scaring him.

As all this was going through my mind, I saw my dad drop a cigarette butt on the floor and step on it. Luckily, I don't think anyone saw him. I quickly got up and met him as he walked toward me. "Dad, you can't do that."

"Look, Son, stop telling me what to do. I'm still your father!"

Same old Dad, thank goodness.

"Don't give me a damn reason to say anything. Stay over in the designated spot until you're done smoking, please," I replied.

He mumbled "all right" as he walked away from me and sat down on his mattress.

I looked at him for a minute or so and then walked over. "Hey look, Dad. I'm sorry if you think I keep telling you what to do; it's just that in here we've gotta follow the rules with no exceptions. We're in here with a bunch of other folks, and they're on edge."

"All right. I didn't realize what I was doing until you said something. Sorry, I'm just ready to go."

"Me too, Buddy. As soon as I find anything out I'll let you know."

As he turned his head to look out the window, the bathroom door slammed again. My dad yelled, "Why the hell does everyone keep slamming the door?"

"I haven't got a clue, Dad. I'm gonna go get some paper and put a sign on the door."

I went over to the second floor clinic. It was still dark as a coalmine. I asked if anyone was in there and got no response. I went back to get a flashlight so I could find some paper, tape, and a pen, then I went back to my half-inflated mattress and made two signs; one for the front of the door and one for the back of the door.

They both read, "PLEASE DON'T SLA.M THE DOOR!" Simple and to the point.

After taping the signs to each side of the door, a little old black lady came up and thanked me. "Thank you Son ... I hope this works. That damn banging is really getting on my nerves. Really unnecessary — all that bangin', you know?"

"You're welcome, ma'am. Spread the word. Maybe people will be more considerate."

I went over to the doorway by the recreational area. Before I got there, I saw Nurse/Deputy Robert and a few other people going through the stairwell that leads to the 10th floor. Curious, I followed after them, lagging behind. To my surprise, they went through the door at the mezzanine level. I followed and when I got in there they were on the roof area again. I went out and saw there were a few people walking around surveying the area.

I asked Robert what was going on and he said, "They're startin' to evacuate the inmates to the Broad Street Bridge, and then upstate."

Even more curious, I asked, "Where? To Angola or something?"

"Angola, Hunts, all over the South, probably."

"What building are they starting with?"

"TP I, II, III, and IV first, then probably OPP (Orleans Parish Prison). I'm not really sure."

"When will they move our building?"

Robert turned to me with a blank, uncertain look on his face. "Probably last, because we're on the second floor and the water hasn't gotten up to our floor yet, unlike some of the other buildings."

I looked down at the water surrounding our building. I wondered how high it had to get before they moved us. It was getting close to 11 a.m., and the day was becoming a real scorcher. With the oppressively humid August weather and no sign of a cloud in the sky to protect us, we were getting the full brunt of the sun beating down.

I stared at the thick smoke coming right over our building. It appeared to be coming from the Mississippi River area. When I walked back downstairs, I asked a couple people if they knew where the smoke was coming from, but no one did. There was an older African-American gentleman sitting by the break room, listening to the radio.

"Excuse me, sir. Have you heard anything about a huge fire or explosion?"

"Can't say that I have, Son."

"Thanks anyway."

I went back over by my dad to see how he was doing. He was lying down, drenched in sweat and looking overheated.

"You feelin' all right, Dad?"

"I don't know. I feel a little dizzy. I don't know if it's from the heat or what."

"Do you want me to check your blood pressure?" He started to sit up, then immediately laid back down.

"Don't move. I can check it while you're lying down. I'll be right back."

I hustled over to the second floor clinic, grabbed a blood

pressure cuff and stethoscope and took his blood pressure. It was a little elevated and his pulse was too. I helped him to his feet and took his blood pressure again. It was still mildly elevated, but his pulse was bounding at 104 beats a minute. This was possibly a sign of mild dehydration, so I explained this to him and got him to drink a bottle of water.

Helping him lay back down, I told him to relax and grabbed my pillow and fanned him with it. "That's not necessary, Son. You don't have to."

Not thinking twice, I said, "I don't mind. Hey, how many blood pressure pills do you have left?"

"Five or so."

I told him I went upstairs earlier to the clinic to see if we had his type of blood pressure medicine, but we didn't. "Don't worry," I told him. "I'll talk to one of the doctors to see if there is something comparable that we can substitute."

After a couple minutes of fanning my dad, I told him to drink more water at the first sign of dizziness and to slack off on the smoking.

"I haven't been smoking that much," he said.

I knew he had, but I wasn't going to argue with him.

Nurse Cecelia walked by while I fanned my dad.

"Is he all right?" she asked.

"Yeah, just a little hot and dizzy," I replied.

"If you need anything, let me know."

"Thanks."

I fanned him for about a half-hour more until he fell asleep. I went to stand by the bathroom door to make sure no one would slam it and wake him. The smell was damn awful, but I felt I had to keep the noise down as much as I could so my dad could rest. Standing there, I tried to point out the signs to people as they came and went; especially the younger ones.

People around the room fanned themselves with whatever they could. I know I keep harping on the heat, but it was brutal. No breeze or circulation of air to speak of. I knew elderly people and infants around the city were surely dying from it.

After an hour or so, I decided I needed some fresh air. On my way to the recreational area, I saw Dr. Marcus and two nurses running to the stairwell that leads to the 10th floor. There must have been some sort of emergency, but I didn't have the energy to ask. If I, a young fit man was exhausted, what about women, children, and the elderly all over the city?

The doorway was crowded and a sickly man sat in a wheelchair with a nasal cannula (clear plastic tubing) running to his nose. His oxygen tank was attached to the side of his wheelchair. I couldn't believe my eyes when he took the nasal cannula off his head and lit up a cigarette. He probably had chronic obstruction pulmonary disease or some other respiratory problem, and it was maybe 120 degrees in there, and he lit up a cigarette! We were basically stranded and our supplies were running short. What was he thinking?

After a few minutes of watching this guy, I left to see what was going on out on the roof. Once I got up there, I noticed the number of people had swelled quite a bit. When I walked out the door, I heard a loud swooshing sound so I walked around to investigate the noise. I saw a military helicopter with a Red Cross symbol hovering right above the roof. The wind generated from the helicopter was ferocious and it felt like an oven-hot tornado.

Even so, any wind felt pretty good.

After about two or three minutes of the helicopter looking like it was going to land, it dropped some water and supplies and eased straight up in the air and took off. Deputies moved the supplies back toward to the main part of the roof by the entrance door. Whoever was on the roof was able to take some water if they needed it, so I grabbed a couple of bottles and went back down by my dad.

Some areas of the second floor were active with people and others did not have as much movement. The heat seemed to affect everyone differently. My dad was lying down looking up at the ceiling with his hands behind his head.

"Hey, Buddy, you awake?" I asked.

"Yeah. Damn door keeps slamming. Can't people see the sign?"

"You would think; it's right by the door knob. I stood over there for an hour earlier while you were sleeping so I could stop it from slamming." He acknowledged my efforts with a smile then asked me to look at his back. "It's itching like crazy!" When I removed his shirt I saw that he had a bad heat rash or something.

"Let me go get some hydrocortisone cream to help with the itching." The second floor clinic didn't have any, so I took the stairs to the 10th floor. Winded, I stopped on the eighth floor to catch my breath. When I got to the 10th floor, I looked out the window and saw what looked like at least a dozen military helicopters in the air in a square formation. It looked like they were hovering, doing some sort of surveillance. It was strange to see the military presence, but I was glad to see them. After watching this for a few minutes, I searched the supply room and found a couple of tubes of hydrocortisone cream.

Exhausted and running on adrenaline, I eventually got back to our area just in time to see my dad trying to scratch his back with his shoe.

Moving behind him I said, "Pull your shirt up or off and I'll rub this cream on your back." I know it must have looked pretty funny, rubbing this cream on his back while his old man boobs jiggled around. I hate to knock the old man, but his man-boobs *are* droopy.

I was snickering to myself a little bit and he heard me, "What's so funny? What's so funny?"

"This is. Rubbing cream on your back, in a jail, in sweltering heat when you could have been sitting on a couch at your sister's house in the air conditioning!"

With a half-hearted smile he said, "I guess you're right.

Don't rub it in!" We both laughed as a young teenage girl walked by crinkling her nose while giving us a peculiar look.

After covering his back, I told Dad to lie on his side and I would fan his back with the pillow. I fanned him for quite a while and eventually I was covered with sweat. I grabbed a chair nearby and sat down and took my shirt off, continuing to fan him until he was sound asleep. I don't really remember how long I fanned him, but the next thing I knew I fell out the chair, landing on my right knee and elbow on my now deflated mattress.

"Ouch! Damn!" My dad didn't hear me since he was sound asleep. I got up, grabbed my towel, and wiped the sweat from my arms, chest, and face.

It looked like my dad wasn't breathing.

His mouth was slightly open and he was lying on his side. I watched for about 10 more seconds and still no breath. I didn't want to wake him up if he was sleeping, but for a moment I wasn't sure. I got a sinking feeling and then a panicking feeling. Just as I was about to shake him, he took a big, deep breath through his nose and mouth, making a loud snoring noise.

I jumped back a little and breathed a sigh of relief.

I don't know why I thought the worst at this moment, but I did.

I decided to take a bottle of water and my towel and try to clean myself up a little bit. Turning toward the stench factory bathroom, I saw Dr. Marcus walking toward me, holding his right hand around his wrist with his left hand. It looked as if it was totally limp or broken. I could see he was in pain, but it looked more like he was in shock.

"What happened to your hand, Doc?"

"An Epi-Pen went through my hand and it's totally numb!"

An Epi-Pen is an injection used when someone is having a severe asthma attack and can't breathe. It is a measured dose of epinephrine that helps open the airways so the person having the attack can breathe normally.

"How the hell did that happen?"

"We went up to the fourth or fifth floor, I really don't know, because someone was having an asthma attack from the heat. We couldn't get his condition under control. It was dark as hell on the tier. There were inmates standing all around, and when I grabbed the Epi-Pen and took the top off I almost dropped it. Luckily, or I guess in this case unluckily for me, I had the wrong end in my hand. When I went to jam the needle in his thigh, it went right through my hand."

At this point, he showed me how far the needle had gone through the other side of his hand. "It felt like a gunshot going right through my hand."

With a grimace on my face, I said, "Damn, Doc; did it hit any bones?"

"I don't believe so, but I really couldn't tell you right now because my whole hand is numb." He grabbed his wrist and started to shake his right hand. "It feels like the numbness is going up my arm."

In his defense, an Epi-Pen is flush on both sides and the needle doesn't extend out until pressure is applied to the injection. So if he couldn't see the pen, it's not surprising he accidentally injected himself.

"Is there anything I can do?"

He smiled and said, "You could help me take a leak."

I did a double take look at him, "Do what?"

He started to laugh and said, "Just kidding, Gavin!"

"Good! Because you would've been on your own there."

"No, seriously, I just need to take a nap. I haven't really slept since Monday night, and that wasn't enough sleep."

"Where's your stuff?" I asked.

"I only have a couple of things. When I left Templeman I and II, I left some stuff over there. The water was rising so fast we had to get out of there!"

"Do you have anything to sleep on?"

"Nope."

"Let me go see if I can find you a mattress."

"Oh, that's all right. I'll just sleep by you all on the floor."

"Doc, please let me try to find you something, a mattress or something. In the meantime, use my half-ass air mattress." By this point, my mattress was fairly flat, but at least I wasn't sleeping directly on the floor.

I went to the Watch Office to see if there were any mattresses left. Ms. Sandra, a control deputy, said to check with one of the ranking officials. I looked for 20 minutes or so and couldn't find a soul. I went up to the roof again and there were plenty of people up there. I saw Robert, and he said he didn't know where I could get a mattress for the doctor. As he was walking away I asked, "Any word on leaving yet?"

"I heard maybe tomorrow morning if not sooner."

"Oh, that's great! I'll see you later."

I decided to go try and clean up a little now that I had a chance. My dad was still sleeping and but only taking a breath every 10 seconds or so. Maybe he had sleep apnea. I still felt the need to watch him for a minute or so to make sure he was breathing okay. I couldn't escape the steady paranoia that I was feeling.

I didn't want my dad to die in there.

The bathroom was horrible by now. Thank God they broke out the window or it would have been completely unbearable. I took my bottle of water and poured some of it over my head and onto my towel. I scrubbed my head and wiped off my arms and neck. I looked up into the mirror and saw that my hair looked like I stuck my finger in a light socket. I took my hand and ran it through my hair and to my dismay I had quite a few hairs in my hand.

Great! I'm gonna start losing my hair on top of everything else.

I did it again with the same result. I remembered my longtime friend, Ron, telling me, "Don't worry big boy, when you turn 33 it'll start coming out!" Well, I turned 33 the month before the hurricane.

Dammit! Standing there with no shirt on, hair in my hand, no real shower in five days, and a sewer for a bathroom, I walked out not feeling so good.

This was getting to me.

After a few minutes of self-pity, I changed my shirt and put some shorts on. It was past my time to go up to work, but I really didn't care. The situation had unraveled and no one seemed to be following a schedule at this point. There were rumors we were going to get paid only for regular work shifts, and that ticked everybody off. Here we were, sacrificing ourselves to work under those horrid conditions, and we might not even get fully compensated for our time.

While I was looking in my bag for a pair of socks, my dad woke up. At first he looked a little disoriented, like he didn't know we were still in Hell.

"You up?"

"Umm... yeah. What time is it?"

"After three o'clock, I guess." He sat up and put on his glasses. He was sitting there in just his boxer briefs looking exhausted. "You feelin' all right, Dad?"

"Fine. Just hot as heck."

"Does your back still itch, Dad?"

"Here and there, but not too bad. That cream worked pretty good."

"Good. Are you hungry or thirsty?"

"I need to take my medicine, so I'll drink some water."

"Look at the end of your mattress, I put a bottle down there."

As he leaned forward to grab the bottle of water, he spilled his pills all over the end of his mattress. "Dammit!" he yelled. I helped him pick up his pills. I could tell that he was a little embarrassed.

"Don't worry about it, Dad."

"I'm not worried about it, Son, I got it." It was a common theme between my dad and me during the past few years. He was beginning to make more mistakes and forget things, and he didn't want to admit it. I know he didn't want me to impose on his independence and I never would. I hadn't gotten to see him as much as I did before I got married, but I tried to call him every day. After spending those days together, I realized he really was getting older and starting to slip a bit. Physically, he's in pretty good shape, but mentally he was starting to show his age.

"Do you want me to fix you something to eat?"

"Not right now. I'm so damn hot I don't feel like eating anything."

"I have to go up to work in a little while and I don't know how long I'll be up there, so if you need anything, just ask somebody."

"I'll be fine, Son; just do me a favor and rub a little more of that cream on my back before you leave."

As I rubbed the cream on his back, I looked out the window, and the water seemed like it was getting even higher. The storm was long gone, but the water was not.

113

"This is unbelievable!"

"What's unbelievable Son?"

"Oh ... nothing, Dad ... I was just thinking out loud."

At this time Dr. Marcus was waking up; he looked very pale and appeared as if he was going to throw up. "Doc, you all right?"

"I don't think so ... my kidneys ... my kidneys and bladder are really hurting. Walking and swimming in all that toxic water the past couple of days might have gotten me sick."

I tried to lighten the mood. "Is there anything I can do besides help you take a piss?"

With a forced smile, he replied, "Can you go get me some Bactrim DS please?" Bactrim is an antibiotic commonly used for many infections, usually kidney or urinary tract ones.

"Sure, let me finish here and I'll go get you some."

My dad turned to look at the doctor and saw how bad he looked. "Son, that's fine. Go get those pills for the doctor."

Before I left, I introduced the doc and my dad. Dr. Marcus said, "You have a good son there. I don't know too many sons who would do what he's doing there."

Smiling, my dad said, "Yeah. I'm pretty lucky to have a son like him."

After wiping the excess cream off of my hands, I went over to the clinic. At some time during the day, they took all of the medications out of the carts and put them in garbage bags just like we did on the 10th floor. I asked one of the nurses, who was sitting in there in the dark, if she knew where the Bactrim was.

"Dr. Marcus needs some Bactrim. He thinks he might have a kidney infection or something."

"Look in that bag right there. There might be some in there." After looking through the whole bag, I didn't find what I needed. It took me looking through two more bags before I finally found some.

It was about this time Captain Stanfield, a rank official from the Intake Processing Center, walked in. He looked awful. He said, "I need a tetanus shot or some antibiotics, because I feel like hell. I've been in the water and flat boat for over 40 hours straight."

The few nurses in the second-floor clinic shined their flashlights around and looked at each other in disbelief as he continued. "We've been out in the water saving people and bringing them to higher ground. I have little cuts all over my body and that water is nasty!"

While he continued to tell us about the horrors he had seen in the last day and a half, a nurse and a doctor came to look at Stanfield. The doctor said it was all right to give him a tetanus shot and told one of the nurses to give him some Keflex (an antibiotic) four times a day for seven days. After a few more minutes of listening to what was going on out there, I decided to go back over by Dr. Marcus. He was lying on his back in obvious pain.

"Here you go, Doc. Do you need something to drink?"

"Yes, please, please if you have anything."

"I have some room-temperature water if you want it," I said.

"That'll work."

"All right, guys, I'm heading up to 10, see you later," I said.

I started on my way to the 10th floor. I almost got to the stairwell, and I realized I forgot to tell my dad we might be leaving sometime that evening or the next morning. He appeared to be somewhat relieved when I told him.

The 10th floor was busy. There were two inmates sitting on the bench having their vital signs taken and another one in the medical office having stitches removed. I got a report from the day nurse; there wasn't much out of the ordinary going on. She told me to expect the inmates to be complaining a bit that evening, because all they got to eat that day was one sandwich and no water.

I decided to walk the tier on the north side, which turned out to be a mistake. As soon as I went down there, the inmates started bombarding me.

"This is bullshit!"

"We need something to drink! Where's our food? We're starving in here!"

"What y'all tryin' to do to us, kill us?"

"Our toilets don't work! This is nasty up in here!"

I could feel myself getting really tensed up so, I got everyone's attention. "Listen up! Hey, listen up! We're doing the best we can under the circumstances. The city is real fucked up! They have dead bodies floating all over the city! People are stranded on rooftops and attics out there. People are getting shot, raped, and attacked! You name it, it's happening. Half the city is on fire! I know this sucks, but it sucks for all of us! We're short on food just like y'all."

At this point, a couple of jerks blurted out, "Y'all probably holdin' the food for yourselves!"

"Y' all don't give a shit about us!"

I was really getting angry by then, "Y'all can believe what the hell you want to believe! I'm just tellin' you the way it is! The military looks like its takin' over the city. I would think they are goin' to get us supplies when they can." I was saying this, but I really wasn't sure.

I stood there for a few minutes looking, listening, and answering as many questions as I could. I could see some of those guys were really scared.

"Man, I need to speak to my people."

"Where them levees broke at? My grandma lives over by one of them levees."

Other inmates continued to bitch and complain, and nothing I said made any difference. I saw Nurse Favis out of the corner of my eye, so I just walked away from the tier and blocked out all of the yelling and screaming.

Favis was in the medical office pressing all kinds of buttons on her phone. I watched her do this for a couple of minutes.

"Who are you trying to call?" I asked.

Laughing a little, she said, "I'm trying to use my text messaging on my phone to send a message to my mom, but it's not going through. Somebody downstairs was able to use theirs earlier on the roof." I grabbed my pockets for my phone, but realized it was downstairs in my bag. I asked, "I wonder if I can do that on my phone. I haven't tried it yet."

After making the rounds on the tiers and getting the same response from just about everybody, I went downstairs to get my phone. I hadn't eaten all day and was pretty hungry. The good side to that was I didn't use the bathroom, which made it worth it.

It was around 5 p.m. by the time I got to my bag. My dad was eating raviolis out of a can. When I saw that, my hunger level went down a notch. "I can't see how you could ea t that without heating it up. That looks gross."

Looking at me, he said, "It's so damn hot in here already, you don't need to heat anything up." He had a point there. Just about everyone was down to shorts and a T-shirt.

Some people were down to their underwear, which was a little disgusting.

I could hear the sounds of babies crying in the distance. With the sun beating down on the building all day, staying inside was just about intolerable. The second floor was like a big kiln. No air was circulating at all. Even though we were near one of the only windows, it didn't help. I'm sure at some point there were people suffering from heat exhaustion, and I wasn't going to be surprised if we had a death or two from the heat before it was all over.

I grabbed my cell phone and told my dad I was heading back upstairs. With his mouth full of raviolis, he nodded and waved bye to me. Making that trip up the stairs was getting harder and harder.

Going off pure adrenaline by then, I felt like I was going to pass out when I got to the 10th floor. After each trip, it took longer to catch my breath.

After a few minutes of deep breathing, I turned my phone on. Still no signal or indication that it was going to work. I asked Favis if she had had any luck, and she said "no."

I went into the area where the St. Bernard deputies were so I could listen to the radio. The mood was still somber, obviously, but there were periods of anger voiced by several local political officials throughout the broadcast.

While listening to the radio, I heard the police chief of Kenner (where I live), describing the aftermath of the storm. "I'm riding down Williams Boulevard, and the water is anywhere from three to six feet high. We're turning west on Vintage Drive and the water level appeared to be six feet at one time, based on the water line on the buildings ..." Of all the streets he could have been on he was about two to three blocks from my condo! I now had confirmation that my home was flooded along with my car.

The situation was getting grimmer by the hour. I began to wonder what my dad's place was like. I knew his car was swamped. If his home was too, this was going to be a complete disaster. If my Aunt Gladys' house was flooded, we wouldn't have any other place to stay in the metropolitan area. I had no idea where we would live or where my dad would live. As I was contemplating this, a message popped up on my phone. I heard a beep, and it vibrated a little bit; the only time it usually does that is when I have my phone on silent and I get a phone call. I saw I had a text message. I had never used text messaging before, so said to Favis, "Hey, look at this. Please show me how to get the message."

She took the phone and pressed a couple of buttons and showed me the screen. It said, "R U OK. WE MISS U AND LOVE U. LORA AND FAMILY." I immediately felt a surge of energy.

"Look at that Favis. How do I respond back?"

She showed me and told me when you send a message, a confirmation statement pops up on the screen when it goes through. I tried to message my wife's phone, but the screen said, "Message failed." I tried again with the same results.

"Hey, Favis, why is this not working?"

"Sometimes the signal may not be strong enough or the number you're messaging isn't in a place where it can receive it."

"Great. That figures," I replied.

"Is your phone working?"

"No G; I'm gonna try tomorrow if we're still here. Hopefully, we'll be outta here!"

"I hope so, but they haven't even moved any of the inmates in here yet." She looked at me with a shrug and a forced smile and said, "Oh well."

We sat there in silence for a few minutes. I could hear the occasional inmate asking for this or that and the radio announcer talking about the devastation in and around the city. I decided to go down to the roof of the mezzanine level to see if my text messaging would work.

The sun was setting, and the moon was visible in the distance. Some stars started to gleam and twinkle. The black smoke from the explosion still flowed in the sky. The other fires visible from the mezzanine roof still burned. There were fewer military helicopters than earlier in the day, but I could still hear them flying around. There were empty bottles of water on the roof scattered in an area near the entrance. I walked to the far left-hand part of the roof to see if I could get a signal. I tried my wife's number, but it didn't work. I decided to scroll through my phone list to get my sister-in-law and brother -in-law's phone numbers to see if they would work. On my second try, I got Brian's (my brother-in-law) number to work and I sent a message. It read, "IM OK. DAD OK 4 NOW. VERY HOT AND MISERABLE. LOVE U, GAVIN."

After three tries, I finally got a confirmation message. At that point, I assumed my family got the message. As I went to go back inside, I saw Robert, and he said, "Be ready to go in the morning! You can only bring one bag, and they may not let you bring anything. Pack one bag just in case they let you take one."

Feeling positive for the first time in awhile, I replied, "All right. Thanks! We'll be ready."

I decided to go down and tell my dad the good news. When I got down there, the diesel smell had taken over the second floor.

It was dark but tubes of light from flashlights shined around like lasers. The news of our possible departure in the morning had everyone talking. When I got to my dad, he was smiling. "I guess you heard we might be leaving in the morning?"

"Finally. This heat is killing me!"

"Have you been drinking some water, Dad?"

"Yeah, but I could sure go for a cup of coffee."

"Hopefully wherever they bring us, we can get you some coffee."

"Do you need anything?"

"No, Son. I'm all right. I hope I can get my medicine tomorrow wherever we go."

"That would be nice, Dad, but I wouldn't count on it."

After about a minute or so, it dawned on me I had to decide what to take and what to leave behind. Looking at my dad through the candlelight I said, "Hey, we can only take one bag each, so I'm going to stuff as much as I can in my blue duffel bag and you can put what you want in my black duffel bag. We'll just leave your old suitcase behind." It was old as dirt anyway.

With a mildly disappointed look on his face, he replied, "I guess so. Whatever we have to do to get the hell out of here I'll do it! Hell, I'll walk out of here with no clothes on if I have to."

Laughing and getting a quick (bad) visual image, I mockingly said, "That won't be necessary, but thanks for letting me know that."

I started to rearrange what I thought we would need, changing my mind a couple of times. I had my father-in-law Gary's movies, about 20 or so, and my portable DVD player and was torn whether to take them or leave them behind. After a couple of minutes, I decided to just pack them in the bag as tightly as I could.

I took my other duffel bag and put my dad's stuff and the rest of my things in there. While I was packing, I heard on the radio people, I assumed looters or gangs, were shooting at military helicopters trying to land on top of hospitals, mainly Charity. I couldn't believe what I was hearing! It was odd.

Here I am in a jail and I feel safer than if I were out in the open somewhere in the city.

With all the lawlessness and turmoil, at least our criminals were behind bars, for now.

After picking up each bag, I was hoping I wouldn't have to walk too far because they were quite heavy. I decided to leave my pillow (of course my favorite pillow) and the air mattresses behind, plus a few pieces of clothing. I thought I'd better go back up to the 10th floor to see if anything was going on. Since the first night, things had been crazy at times and relatively quiet at times, thank God. We obviously didn't have the capabilities to treat a life-or-death situation, and the facility was unable to access local hospitals.

Just before I went upstairs, I saw Nurse Urban's mother entering the bathroom with a box of gloves and cleaning supplies in her hands. I couldn't believe my eyes. She was actually going to clean that toxic cesspool of a bathroom. Anybody who would voluntarily do that deserves a Medal of Honor. I offered her the choice of anything I had to eat, "When you're done just look in this orange bag here. Take whatever you want."

With her Latin accent, she said, "Oh, tank you berry mooch. You berry kind."

I told my dad, "She's cleaning the bathroom; let her have anything she wants to eat."

"She's cleaning *that* bathroom?! Hell. She can have all of it if she wants. Wow!" My dad and I both looked at each other and shook our heads. I don't know how long it took her to do it and I almost gag every time I think of her cleaning that filth!

I told my dad I was going back upstairs for a while and I would see him later. I stopped on the mezzanine level to look outside. Walking out on the roof was like stepping into a whole new world: The night sky took my breath away. For a second straight night, the sky was completely illuminated with stars. It looked like there were more stars in the sky than darkness.

It felt so surreal, as if I were in outer space. Standing there looking straight up, I again had that strange, spiritual feeling of a higher power controlling all of it. New Orleans had been so screwed up for so long, maybe divine intervention was the only way it was going to get fixed. With all of the corrupt politicians, judges, and criminals, maybe this event might be what was needed to get things turned around.

A cleansing?

It's a shame, because a lot of good people were suffering, but maybe it would get all the crooks to keep their hands out of the cookie jar. I could only hope. There are many good things about New Orleans, but the bad sometimes outweighs the good.

I stood there a little longer thinking. It was all happening so fast, yet being there, everything was in slow motion. A few seconds later I heard the crackle of gunfire in the distance. I instinctively ducked down and covered my head; maybe this roof wasn't the best place to be at night. Turning to go back upstairs, I ran into Deputy Rico. He was with his family. Believe it or not, with the moonlight and the brightness of the stars, it was possible to make out figures and see a little bit.

"Hey, Gavin ... come meet my family."

Deputy Rico recently moved to New Orleans from California and was new to the hurricane experience. He sure picked a heck of a hurricane start with. Anyhow, he made a decision earlier in the day to bring his family on the roof and let them sleep out there for the night. It was kind of like camping without the trees and wildlife, unless you consider what was going on in the city as wildlife.

"Gavin, this is my wife ... my daughter ... my son ... and my ..." All in all, he had about seven or eight people with him and they were all set up on the roof with sleeping bags and pillows.

"You got 'em all set real good up here."

"Yeah, it sure beats the inside. It's getting miserable in there!"

I said, "Getting miserable? It's downright pitiful! You see the bathroom lately?"

"Unfortunately, I have, and it's unbelievable."

"Urban's mom had started to clean it up when I was on my way up here."

His jaw nearly hit the ground.

"You're kidding. That's unreal."

"I wouldn't have believed it if I didn't see it with my own eyes." After a few more minutes of small talk, I told him I had to go back upstairs.

I thought about asking my dad if he wanted to come up to the roof, but then thought better of it. I had mental images of him wandering around in the middle of the night and falling off the side of the building into the water, never to be seen again.

When I got to the 10th floor, the inmates were chanting, ranting and raving. Favis was sitting in the office with the door closed. She just smiled and said, "They're getting louder and louder with that crap."

It was about 9:15 p.m. or so and I was about fed up with dealing with the inmates. I understood their frustration, but we were all in the same boat. No matter what we said they didn't believe us, so what was the use of trying to explain the situation anymore?

J.W. seemed to be doing all right — physically, but he really didn't comprehend what was going on.

I made the mistake of letting him see me, and he shouted, "Dad, when are we going home?"

I hesitated for a second or two before I answered, because I could see he was sincere.

"J.W. listen, we've had a real bad rainstorm and it's flooded outside. They're going to move us to somewhere where it's not flooded." I could hear someone laughing because I was talking to him like a kid, but that was his state of mind. I turned to the guy who was laughing and said, "Will you shut the hell up, man?"

"Yeah man. I was just playin'," he replied.

"Not right now please. Thanks." J.W was waiting for me to continue. "Like I was saying J.W., we're going to be leaving soon. You're going to be all right."

He told me to come close to the cell so he could whisper. "Are you coming with me?" Not wanting to upset him, I said, "Probably so ... go lie down and try to get some sleep, okay?"

"All right, Dad, see you later!"

I went back into the office for a little while and tried to use my text messaging with no success. I was listening to the radio and I heard the announcer say, "The Gentilly and New Orleans East area is inundated with water. Anywhere from eight to ten feet of water covering the area ..." My heart sank in my chest thinking of the fertility clinic where our embryos were frozen in New Orleans East. There was a real possibility everything was now flooded, maybe even destroyed. I just put my head down and prayed everything would be all right. Along with everything else potentially lost, this would be the hardest to deal with.

"Hey Favis, I'm heading downstairs. I've had enough for today. I'll see if Urban will come up early."

"Okay, G, that's cool. See ya later." I went back downstairs to the second floor. When I got to our spot , it was very dark with the only light coming from a candle on the table. It was the same candle with the image of Jesus on it. Dr. Marcus, Urban, his mother, my dad, and Dr. Singh were sitting and lying around. Urban saw me and said, "Aren't you supposed to be up on 10 right now?"

"Yeah, but I had enough of that today; besides Favis is up there and it's fairly quiet, except for the complaining and occasional chanting."

Looking concerned, Urban said, "Does she need any help?"

"I told her I'd see if you would want to go up there early. Would you?"

He looked at his watch and said, "It's only ten after ten. I'll go up in about half an hour."

I changed my shirt and sprayed on some deodorant; I was sure I smelled pretty bad. I tried lying down on my deflated mattress and shot back in frustration. "I just bought this stupid air mattress and it ain't worth damn!" I lifted up my mattress and used Urban's flashlight to see why it was deflated. Everything looked good until I spotted a little sliver of glass from the shattered window. I couldn't see a hole in the mattress, but it most likely came from broken glass. *That figures. I guess I'll just lay out some clothes and sleep on them!*

Once I got settled in, we all started talking. I don't remember how we got on the subject, but we started talking about where the inmates were going. Someone said, "That's gonna' be screwed up if someone is in here on a drunk in public charge and now they'll be somebody's "girlfriend" up at Angola." We all burst out laughing.

Dr. Marcus chimed in next, "So if somebody was arrested for a traffic violation, they're going to end up at Angola Penitentiary?"

"Possibly," I said. "I know we have a couple people who were scheduled to roll out Monday. They'll end up at Angola too."

Dr. Singh just looked at us under the soft candlelight with a smirking smile and said, "You guys are terrible." She was right. But it was sort of humorous — so long as it wasn't us.

We continued entertaining ourselves with different scenarios that might play out for the unlucky souls who were leaving our facility. Then Dr. Marcus brought us up to date on the evacuation of the Medical Observation Unit and told us how some of the medical staff couldn't swim, so they had to use garbage cans and benches to float the medical staff to the CCC building. As the conversation slowed down, Urban left to go up to the 10th floor, and I could see that my dad was starting to dose off.

"Hey, Dad, good night. Love you, Buddy."

"Good night, Son. Love you." Soon he was asleep.

Chapter Seven

EVEN THOUGH OUR BUILDING WASN'T
EVACUATED YET, I was feeling pretty confident we would be
leaving the next day. Trying to cool down, I took my sweaty shirt off.
Even at 11 p.m., everybody was sweating profusely, and the only way
to generate any breeze was to fan myself with something. I grabbed
the pillow in the middle and started fanning my dad again.

I found myself staring at the candle on the table. The way it
was flickering it seemed to project the Jesus-like image on the wall.
The candle had some Spanish writing on it, and I'm not sure if it was
Jesus or not. Still, it was oddly comforting.

I felt myself smiling at the candle, and every time I did, it
seemed like the flame got brighter and the image on the wall got
bigger. I don't know if I was hallucinating from the heat, but when I
wasn't smiling the flame didn't appear as bright or the image as big. It
changed when I smiled or looked at it and it always got brighter and
bigger. I did this for a while, becoming somewhat mesmerized by this
mystical occurrence. Peculiar, I know.

Just about everyone was sleeping. I noticed the smell from the
bathroom wasn't as bad as before. Nurse Urban's mother must have
really done a great job. God bless her!

For the next hour or so, I continued fanning my dad and trying to block out the sound of occasional gunshots in the distance.

The way things had gone so far, I was hoping no stray bullets would find their way through our windows. By this time, I was thinking of all kinds of crazy scenarios.

I decided to eat a granola bar since I hadn't had anything to eat all day. While munching on it and drinking room temperature, in this case *hot*, water, I caught myself looking at the candle again and again. The flame would get brighter and brighter. I got chills on my neck, and a calming feeling came over me. It seemed otherworldly. I truly felt a supernatural presence. After a while, I turned over to try and get some sleep on my bed of lumpy clothes.

I don't know what time it was in the morning, but it was still dark. I was half asleep when I felt someone shaking my left arm and whispering my name, "Gavin ... Son, wake up." I sat up, one of my clammy shirts stuck to my face. I was covered with sweat and the stench from the bathroom was back.

"Son, I gotta go to the bathroom."

Trying to get my bearings I said something like, "Let me grab the flashlight, and I'll go with you."

I tore off part of the remaining piece of sheet, grabbed a roll of toilet paper and told my dad to hold on to my shoulder and follow the light. He fumbled with his eyeglasses a bit, but got them on. I had to hold in a laugh because when he stood up, his hair was standing straight up on the left side of his head and all he had on was his boxer shorts and a pair of my flip-flops, which were a little too small.

We tip-toed our way to the bathroom and when we got in there, I saw this five gallon bucket with a rope tied to the handle and the other end of the rope tied to a leg of the counter where the sinks were. I went over to the toilets and saw the bad news. It hadn't taken long for the bathroom to get back to its crappy state. It was amazing to me so many people had such little respect for the facility and everyone else there. I looked up and saw a sign on the door that said, "NO PAPER IN THE TOILET!" I said to myself, *No paper in the toilet ... that's all they had in the toilets in addition to you know what."*

Then my dad said, "What are you doing, Son?"

"I'm trying to figure out what to do ... you can't go in either one of these."

I looked at the bucket and looked at the sheet in my hand and said, "Here's your toilet right here." I took the sheet and tore enough to line the bucket. "All right, Dad, have a seat."

Looking tentative, he said, "I don't know, Son. I don't know if I can go in that."

"Well, that's your only choice right now, everything else is too nasty and you could get sick. So give it a try." I helped him get positioned on the bucket and stepped over by the door to give him his privacy.

After he finished, he said, "Well, Son, I've never done that before." We laughed and took the sheet and wrapped the little present up and threw it out the window. The way I saw it, we really didn't have a choice.

We went back to our spot and my dad laid back down. I grabbed my pillow and fanned him until he fell back asleep. I didn't get to see what time it was, but it was still dark outside. Before I knew it, I was asleep.

I awoke to loud voices outside the window; I could hear boat motors going and what sounded like people giving commands.

"DON'T MOVE! DO AS WE SAY!"

"KEEP YOUR HANDS WHERE WE CAN SEE THEM!"

I looked out the window, and every few minutes I saw a small flat boat go by with inmates in the middle and armed guards sitting on the edges. I decided to go up to the mezzanine to take a closer look.

When I got up there, I saw Nurse Robert and asked him if we were getting ready to leave. "Not yet. It may not even be today. I really don't know."

Deflated, I said, "You're kidding, right?"

"Nope. It's taking along time to move the inmates by boat. We can only get six to eight per boat and you know we got somethin' like six thousand to seven thousand inmates to move."

With my tone changing to exasperation I said, "Damn! I was sure we were leaving today."

I guess he could see I was frustrated, "Hang in there G. How's your dad?"

"Okay right now, but he thought we were leaving today. Plus, he's just about out of his medicine ."

Looking like he really didn't know what to say, he replied, "I don't know what to tell you, dude. We're doin' the best we can."

"Oh, I know. Don't worry about it. I'll talk to you later." Robert walked away, repositioning his rifle and scratching his backside in the same motion.

I walked over by the south side of the roof and I could see inmates in boats. The Templeman buildings had inmates waving white sheets or towels out of the shattered, steel-barred windows and some other inmates sat on the roof with nowhere to go. I looked to my far right, and the CCC building had a window about six stories up with about five or six sheets or blankets tied together hanging out of it. I then looked to my far left toward the Broad Street Bridge, which was about 200 yards away; rows and rows of shackled inmates sat or squatted on the bridge, surrounded by men with guns. I then looked to the right of the inmates on the bridge and down below I could see all types of buses on the I-10 Interstate taking inmates and civilians away. There was some type of ladder or slide set up from the bridge down to the highway below. People got off the boats and walked through the water below the bridge. In the distance, I could hear the loud roar of airboats, sounding like racecars revving their engines. The sky was full of military and Red Cross helicopters. The scene was very apocalyptic.

I walked around the entire roof, taking it all in. I looked at my car one more time, and all I could see was about a foot of the top of it. My dad's car was completely submerged. The water was still rising with no apparent end in sight.

We were at one of the lowest spots in the city and I was at one of the lowest points in my life. It was at that moment I felt as if my dad and I were in Alcatraz Prison surrounded by toxic water, hoping we wouldn't have to swim to *FREEDOM!*

I began to reflect on anything I might have done in my life that would have landed me in this situation.

Was this situation a punishment for my younger, wilder days? I didn't know.

But what did my dad ever do to deserve this at 83? Some things just don't make sense.

I heard the loud roar of a military helicopter and when I was able to see it, I saw the helicopter drop some boxes of MREs, meals ready to eat, and more water. I had mixed feelings at this point, because I was grateful we were getting more supplies, but worried we may not be leaving anytime soon.

After the drop was completed, the people in charge started to organize and hand out supplies. I waited for a little while before I went over to see what they had. They asked, "How many people do you have with you?"

I answered, "My dad and I." I was given two brown plastic bags that were tightly sealed and hard like a box was in the bag. I also got two bottles of water. I took my supplies and went downstairs to see my dad.

When I got to our spot, he wasn't there. I opened one of the MREs to see what was inside. To my surprise, the food looked pretty good: a bag of M&Ms, peanuts, crackers, trail mix, and a main course of lasagna. I looked at it for a moment wondering how good lasagna would be out of a box. I was pretty hungry because I really had not eaten anything except a couple of granola bars the past couple of days. I decided to eat some of the trail mix and save the M&Ms for my dad, since he loves his chocolate.

A few minutes later, he walked up and said he was out of cigarettes. Half jokingly, I said, "Good." He didn't seem amused.

"Don't worry, Dad, give your lungs a break. I'll find you some later."

With an agitated look on his face he said, "Yeah, yeah, whatever," and I left it at that. I decided change the subject a bit and show him the MREs and give him the pack of M&Ms before I told him we were probably not going to leave that day.

While he was eating his M&Ms, I said casually, "It doesn't look like we'll be leavin' today."

He looked at me with total disappointment, "What? You *are* joking, right?"

Looking down, not wanting to make eye contact with him, I said, "Nope, they're still evacuating the other buildings and since only the first floor of our building is flooded and not up here yet, we'll probably be the last building evacuated."

Disgusted and upset he said, "Damn, Son! I guess I won't get my medicine any time soon." He had anxiousness on his face, and I knew there was nothing I could do about it.

"Listen, Dad — we have a couple of doctors here in case you have any problems."

"Yeah, but my meds!"

"I know ... I know. I already talked to one of the doctors and if you start having any trouble, I'm sure that we can give you some other comparable medication."

"I don't know about that, Son."

Trying not to sound perturbed, I replied, "Well, Dad, we really don't have a choice right now, unless you want to swim out of here."

"Could we do that?"

"Are you freakin' kiddin'? Even if we could, all the drug stores are getting looted, you know, broken into, or are on fire!"

Half slapping his leg, he blurted out, "Goddamn! What have I gotten myself into?"

At this point, I didn't say anything. I sat there on the floor and looked out of the nearby shattered window. My dad huffed and puffed for a couple of minutes and finished eating his M&Ms.

"Dad, I'll be back in a little while. As soon as I find out anything I'll let you know. Try and relax."

"Yeah, yeah," he said. And off I went.

It was mid-afternoon, I guess about 2 or 2:30, and I decided to go back to the roof. Once again, it was an extremely hot and muggy summer day, without a cloud in the sky. There were plenty people on the roof now, and some of the deputies guarded a doorway that led to a parking garage next to our building. I found out it was a parking garage for the NOPD and some other vehicles like boats and motorcycles. They were using those vehicles to siphon off gas in order to keep the boats running. I also heard that batteries were being taken for power as well.

Who would have known we had our own looting going on?

Anyhow, the boats, obviously, were the only means of transportation, especially to move the inmates to the nearby bridge for evacuation.

When I was on the roof, Urban's mom, the lady who cleaned the foul bathroom, asked me to help her move some cardboard boxes in to the doorway to the roof because she said there was "aceed" (acid) leaking from the containers in the mezzanine area. I asked her how she knew this and in her strong Spanish accent she said, "Me feet is a burning! Me shoes have been wet and they burning. Help me please cover the floor so no one else feet is burning!" She looked pretty adamant about doing this so we went back down to the second floor and started gathering up old cardboard boxes and anything we could use to cover the floor.

There were some blue tarps near the old cafeteria area and used cardboard boxes in the back of the second-floor medical clinic. Since there wasn't much light in the building, we had to drag the stuff around in the dark. We both tripped a couple times, but, luckily, weren't injured.

Prisoners of Katrina

Once we finally got to the mezzanine area, we started to tear the cardboard boxes long-ways so they could cover more of the floor. There was about an inch or so of water and "acid" on the floor between the bottom of the metal stairs to the doorway. After laying down as many boxes as we could, we laid the tarp down and it covered almost to the doorway to the roof. I thought we were finished, but she said, "Need more! Not enough. We find more." She was small in stature, but had this forceful demeanor about her.

Feeling like I didn't have much of a choice and trying to sound enthused, I said, "All right, let's go."

For the next half-hour or so, we searched the entire second floor for things we could use to cover the walkway. Many people lying or sitting around were looking at us like we were nuts. I let her take the lead and didn't say much. When anyone gave me a strange look, I just shrugged my shoulders and grabbed what I could.

When we finally finished gathering and laying down what we could, it looked like someone had cut open a gigantic trash bag and poured it out in a straight line. It wasn't pretty, but it did the job.

Luckily, I had thick shoes on, so I didn't know what she was feeling on her feet, but I could tell she was having some pain or burning sensation. I gave her a pair of my socks when we were done, and she cleaned her feet with a bottle of water and an old shirt. I'm not sure how many pairs of feet we saved from the "acid" and not many people knew why those boxes, tarps, and other stuff were on the floor, but at least we tried to solve the problem.

It was about mid-afternoon by then, and the heat was wicked. With a minimal breeze up on the roof, it had to be near 100 degrees with 98 percent humidity. After taking a 15-minute break, I went to go check on my dad. He was lying down facing the wall, wearing only his boxer shorts. I thought he was asleep, but he surprised me by calling my name.

"Oh, hey, Dad. I thought you were sleeping."

"It's too damn hot and my back is itching like crazy. My lower back is hurting as well."

"Hang on a second, and I'll rub some of that anti-itch cream on your back." I sat down for a second and drank some warm water and dug around to find the cream.

I was in the middle of putting the cream on his back when Dr. Marcus, Nurse Technician Michelle, and a couple of the nurses rushed to our area near the window by the incoming light. I turned to see what all the commotion was, and I saw Michelle holding her right index finger with a bloody shirt wrapped around it.

Michelle was just about to take her test to be a licensed nurse before the storm and was well on her way to being a great nurse. At some point between Wednesday night and the time she showed up right behind me, they broke out all of the small windows on the 10th floor to help with air circulation. She was up on the ledge looking out the window on the 10th floor and when she jumped down, her hand was on the window and her right index finger snagged a piece of the jagged glass and cut it down to the bone.

Prisoners of Katrina

Her makeshift bandage was completely soaked with blood. She must have cut an artery because blood was squirting out every other second when Dr. Marcus uncovered it.

Her finger looked like a shrimp that had been "butterflied" open, and blood squirted with every heartbeat. The nurses came back with sutures and supplies to stitch up her finger. The cut was so deep Dr. Marcus was concerned about the tendons being permanently damaged and infection setting in. I hurriedly wiped my hands off and told my dad to wait a minute so I could help.

We set up a sterile field (as sterile as we could get the area), and the doc deadened the cut with Lidocaine and began to clean the wound with Betadine antiseptic. He carefully began stitching up the wound. There were a few people standing around watching intently. Michelle couldn't bear to watch. We were joking with each other and I tried to loosen her up with some jokes. "Nice trigger finger. At least you've got four good ones left!" It seemed to calm her down by the few forced laughs she let out.

It took Dr. Marcus 30 minutes or so to close the wound. He asked Nurse Favis to go get her some Keflex (antibiotic) to take in case any infection set in. Dr. Marcus was totally exhausted by this point and was quite proud of his work. "I have to say that was one of the toughest stitch jobs I've ever done. With the cut down to the bone, she really needed surgery, but I think I got it done!" After patting himself on the back for a second, he got serious and said, "I have to warn you that your finger may not come back 100 percent the way it was before, and the risk of infection is quite high."

I could see the concern on her face as she sarcastically replied, "That's great."

Dr. Marcus continued with, "Keep it bandaged up for a couple of days and when you change it, make sure your hands are clean."

She nervously asked, "I'm not going to lose my finger, am I?"

"No, no. Keep taking the antibiotics and keep it clean, and you should be okay."

She didn't look convinced and yelled, "I can't believe this shit!"

Before Favis and another nurse bandaged the finger, I took one last look at it. I think he used 12 to 15 stitches and the wound looked like a small zipper on her finger.

While the other nurses covered the wound, she asked me if I had spoken to the rest of my family lately. "Not since Monday night. I got a text message yesterday and sent one back, but I don't know if they got it."

She looked at me and said, "They have some deputies on the 10th floor who are able to call and get calls."

I looked at her with amazement and asked, "What? How?" Dr. Marcus heard what she said and said something to the same effect.

At about that moment, Dr. Marcus and I stood up and Urban walked up to see what was going on. I went over to my bag to grab some water and said, "I'm going to 10 to see if I can get a hold of Lora!"

Dr. Marcus and Urban simultaneously said, "We're coming too!"

Dr. Marcus then said, "Gavin, can I use your phone when we get up there?"

"Hell yeah, Doc. Lets go!"

When we got to the 10th floor, I saw about 15 deputies with phones in their hands trying to make calls. Deputy Avery was sitting with his head down and his hands on top of his head, looking distraught. "What's up Avery? You all right?"

"No man. I don't know what's up with my girl and my 8-month-old baby boy. The last time I heard their voices was on the radio, and she was calling from the attic of our place."

I didn't quite know what to say. I couldn't imagine a worse scenario for his family. "Where do you live?"

"In the East (New Orleans East), man. In the East." I stood there looking out of the window, feeling awfully bad for him. I waited a couple of minutes before saying, "Man, stay positive. At least her voice went out over the radio. Hopefully, they got help."

"Yeah, thanks G." But I wasn't so sure he was convinced. I waited for a couple of minutes before trying to use my phone.

Everyone was dialing and trying to speak quickly because the signals were fading in and out. One of the female deputies said, "Stand over to your right by the corner and squat down a little bit. You might get a signal." I tried that a couple of times with no luck. Dr. Marcus asked me if he could try my phone. I took a step back and let him get near the corner where I was. He tried for a few minutes with no luck either. Urban had his phone with him and gave it to Dr. Marcus as well. Still no luck.

It's amazing we can build a space station and go to the moon, but we can't keep telephones working here on earth!

Another female deputy offered me her phone. "Hey G, try my phone, but only for a couple of minutes."

"Hey thanks." I tried Lora's cell phone number and on third or fourth ring, she answered, "Hello? Gavin! Gavin!"

"Hey baby, it's me!"

She immediately started crying saying, "Are you all right?

They have ... all kinds of crazy stuff on CNN! Like ..."

"Hey, hey, calm down. I'm all right. What are they saying?"

"They're saying that ... that ... there's a riot at the prison. That they have hostages. That there are people — getting shot!"

Trying to reassure her, I said, "Nothing has happened in this building, yet. It's just miserably hot, and we're surrounded by water. I don't know when we're going to be evacuated. Just know I'm barely making it for now."

She started to cry more, barely catching her breath. "How's your Dad?"

"He's alive. I think he's just hanging in there."

"What do you mean?" Realizing I was not using my phone and other people needed to use it I said, "Nothing ... hey, listen, I'm using someone else's phone. I think this text messaging thing works on my phone — I got a text yesterday from ya'll ... did you get mine?"

"No, no ... you're breakin' up a little."

"I'm okay right now. I'll try to call you later. Love you."

"What. .. I can't hear you"

"I love you! I'll call you later."

I faintly heard her say, "I love you too," and the call was dead.

At that moment I let out a sigh of relief, but then realized neither of us was sure what was going on.

All I knew was our building was secure at that time. Dr. Marcus and Urban were waiting rather impatiently for the phone. I went to hand the phone back to the female deputy and she must have seen the looks on their faces, because she said, "Give it to the Doc!" I turned back around toward Dr. Marcus and she said over my shoulder, "Two minutes, Doc, and you too."

"Oh, Jesus. Thanks."

For the next few minutes both the doc tor and nurse tried to call whoever it was they were trying to call, with no success. I stood there with all kinds of emotions going on. I looked to my left and saw Deputy Avery just looking down with a blank stare on his face.

Another deputy was talking adamantly with a family member about something, another deputy was on her phone laughing about something, and to my right Dr. Marcus was frantically dialing numbers, with no success. Urban was dialing his phone with no success either, but I had been able to at least hear Lora's voice, and she at least knew my dad and I were all right and not hostages.

At least not yet.

I turned to Urban and said, "You're not gonna believe what they're saying on national news. That the jail has been taken over and that there are hostages and riots! Stuff like that!"

With his mouth opening wide he said, "You kidding?"

"That's what she said. Is that freakin' crazy or what? I wonder if something happened in one of the other buildings and they're just not saying anything?"

"Who knows? All I know is I don't think we're leavin' anytime soon."

"I hope you're wrong, but you're probably right."

Just as I was saying that, my phone vibrated in my pocket. I grabbed it and looked at the screen and it read, "WE ALL LUV U AND MISS U; BE SAFE. CALL ME WHEN U CAN. I LUV U VERY MUCH. LORA."

I felt so helpless.

I stared at the screen for a minute, contemplating when we might get out of there. It was noisy, with everyone talking to each other or on the phone. I took my phone and asked one of the female deputies to make sure I was sending my response text correctly. "Do this and press that and that should be it."

I sent back a text saying, "LUV U 2. IM OK. HOPE TO SEE U SOON. GAVIN."

After I sent the message, I got the confirmation "message sent" about 15 seconds later. Dr. Marcus was standing there looking frustrated and Urban looked just plain angry. "Doc, who are you trying to call?"

"Mainly my daughter. She lives in Baton Rouge."

"You wanna try my phone again? You could try to text-message her."

"What's that?"

"Here, I'll show you. Give me the number you're trying to call."

For the next couple minutes, we tried to send text messages for Dr. Marcus and Urban, but unfortunately, neither one went through. I happened to look up at one of the broken windows and saw what looked like a little bloodstain on one of the jagged pieces of glass.

"Hey, were any of you up here when Michelle cut her finger?" I asked.

A couple deputies said "Yeah," and one pointed to the spot I was looking at and said, "She was leaning against the window right there and I don't know what happened, but the next thing I know she was holding her finger and blood was all over her hand."

A couple of other deputies echoed the story, saying blood was everywhere. There were some dried droplets on the floor and on the ledge. I know for a fact those windows are not cleaned very often and are probably filled with all kinds of germs. I hoped nothing bad would happen to Michelle, since there wasn't much we could do if she got seriously ill.

It was after 3:30 p.m. and hot as Hades. I went to go to the back of the 10th floor to look in one of the storage areas to see if there was any Gatorade left. I was last in there on Tuesday and there was about a half a case at that time. When I got to the storage room, the pad lock was broken off and the door was slightly open. The room had been cleaned out. Looted, I guess. I went back over to the barred window area and saw a deputy.

"What happened to the storage door?"

"You know G; it's hot up here. We had to get our drink on!"

"I hear ya ... hey, have you talked to your wife at all?" I asked.

"No, man. I begged her to come here or evacuate, but she didn't want to. I don't know man. I'm tryin' not to think about it."

Remembering his family, I asked, "Don't you have kids?"

"Three, G. Three kids now. I'm prayin' they're gonna be all right."

I was really feeling fortunate. This was the second deputy I talked to who had no idea if his family was alive or dead. "Hey, man, I hope everything will be all right."

"Me too, G. Me too."

Again, I thought of our embryos, what could potentially have been our children. New Orleans East was under water, and the fertility clinic probably was also. Our last in-vitro transfer could be affected. I could only hope the necessary precautions were taken in the event of an emergency. I lowered my head for a minute and prayed. It was so important to us. I wondered if Lora was thinking of them too.

Prisoners of Katrina

I went over to an open space by the window and looked out toward the Broad Street Bridge in the middle of the city. I had to look twice at an area in front of where the inmates were. There were two inmates lying half on their side and face down. "Hey y'all, look at those inmates lying face down on the bridge. You think they have been shot or what?"

Just about everybody looked. One of the male deputies said, "He's been lyin' there for as long as I have been up here. At least two hours." I was trying to see any signs of blood, but it was too far away to tell.

It still looked like organized chaos on the bridge. There were civilians sitting and walking around on one side and hundreds of inmates either sitting or squatting in rows surrounded by some deputies with guns and other military personnel. Helicopters still flew all over the city. The water now covered most of the interstate up to the area under the bridge. Someone went to go get a radio, and as soon as it came on the announcer said, "There are reports of people trying to walk across the Crescent City Connection Bridge and being stopped by the Gretna police on the West Bank side of the bridge. There were even reports of gunfire! I repeat: there are ..." Everybody kind of looked shocked.

Someone shouted, "This is unbelievable man!" We all got quiet and listened to the radio. I really don't remember what else was broadcast, but none of it was good.

After a while, I decided to go back downstairs to check on my dad. I didn't have my flashlight with me, so I just used the handrails and walked down in the dark. Believe it or not, as bright as it was outside, it was just as dark in the stairwell. I was going along, taking my time, but when I got to the sixth floor I started to hear a bunch of male voices barking out commands like, "Don't move! Do exactly as we say! Shut the fuck up! Don't move!"

As I made the turn on the stairwell right before the doorway to the fifth floor tier, I got the scare of a lifetime.

When I stepped off of the last step there was a *jet-black* wolf-looking dog with piercing eyes and gnashing teeth looking right up at me. The only way I was able to see this vicious-looking creature was from the sliver of light coming through the opening tier door.

Attached to a thick leash, it was held back by some sort of armed military-looking man. There were quite a few of those men and then I saw they had "DOC" (Department of Corrections) on their shirts and hats. I stopped dead in my tracks and backed up a few feet against the wall.

It took me a second or two to realize this creature was actually a German Sheppard. I had never seen a one like that. It looked like some sort of wolf dog, but more wolf. Its raven-black coat was extremely shiny and its eyes were bright yellow, with beady pupils. While mesmerized by this animal, I could hear the cell gates opening and orders being yelled at the inmates.

After about 10 seconds of standing very still, the man holding the leash moved forward through the doorway and the dog looked me right in the eye for a second and then went through the door down the fifth floor tier.

Those inmates aren't going to like seeing that scary wolf-dog coming at them!

I couldn't help myself – I took a look down the tier and it was full with men toting sawed-off shotguns, a couple more police dogs, and inmates with their hands on their heads looking extremely scared. One last guy came through the doorway, kind of bumping me out of the way.

I decided I had better get on downstairs before they accidentally lumped me in with the inmates or something. Stepping down the rest of the stairwell, I started having visions of those vicious black dogs tearing me to pieces.

I was getting really unnerved.

When I got to the second floor, most everyone must have realized they were starting to evacuate the inmates. I overheard a group of people say, "We gotta' be gettin' outta' here soon!"

"Yeah, you right."

When I got to my dad, he was eating some crackers, sitting on his mattress looking bored out of his skull.

"Hey, Dad, they're starting to move the inmates out of this building."

"Oh, so we're leaving today?"

"That I don't know. You feelin' all right?"

"I'm getting a little dizzy every now and then. That's about all, other than the heat."

Grabbing my duffel bag and getting my blood pressure cuff and stethoscope, I said, "Sit back against the wall so I can check your blood pressure and pulse."

After positioning his sweaty arm, I placed the BP cuff and stethoscope in position and got a reading of 150/98. High, but not alarming. His pulse was strong and slightly rapid. I figured with the heat and his age, he was probably dehydrated. For that matter, we were all probably dehydrated.

I decided to tell him it was a little lower than it was so he wouldn't worry. Looking at me, he said "Is it all right?"

"Yeah, Dad ... uh, it's not bad. How many pills do you have left?"

Troubled, he said, "One more day's worth."

"We'll be out of here soon."

Looking more disconcerted, he said, "You keep sayin' that, but we're still here!"

"I know, but they're moving the inmates as we speak. Hey, I almost forgot to tell you, I was able to talk to Lora for a couple of minutes upstairs."

"She's upstairs?"

Laughing, I said, "I was able to get in contact with her on the cell phone from the 10th floor. I was able to get some reception up there."

"Oh, is she all right?"

"Yeah. She's in Paris, Texas with family. That is where they evacuated."

"I wish I was in Texas right now."

"Me too, Dad. Me too."

We sat there in silence for a few minutes.

I decided to go up to the mezzanine roof to see what was going on and to find out if we were leaving any time soon. "I'll be back in a minute, Dad."

I went to the roof with the intention of finding Robert to see if he had any new news. On my way there I saw somebody, I can't really remember who, but they said, "I heard we're going to be evacuated to the Convention Center and then onto a Coast Guard ship and brought to Houston."

With my heart sinking in my chest I said, "What? Where did you hear that?"

"One of the rank told me that."

This can't be happening! It's going to take us forever to get there from here, to the Convention Center, on a boat, and then to Houston by boat.

Dejected, I trudged back up to the stairs to the roof to find Deputy Robert. After walking the perimeter of the roof for a few minutes, I saw him standing over by the entry to the adjacent elevated parking lot, where they were siphoning the gas. As I walked toward him, I saw an inmate jumping from an area down to the roof of the other building and then lying on his side, grabbing his leg. There was another inmate sitting near where this inmate jumped to.

Were they making an escape? I wonder where they think they're going... surrounded by water and men with guns.

I made my way over to Robert, and asked him if there was any news. "Not really, Gav. The only thing I do know is that they plan on moving any sick or elderly people first, so your dad ..."

I shot back, "I can't be separated from him! I don't know how he's doing mentally and physically; he could be suffering from dehydration."

"No, no! You would be able to go with him."

"Do you know where?"

"Nope. I've heard all kinds of places — Convention Center, Houma (south Louisiana), Houston, San Antonio."

"Yeah, I heard maybe to the Convention Center, then to Houston on a Coast Guard boat."

"It's possible. Who knows?"

"As long as we get the hell outta' here!"

"I guess you're right. Thanks. I'll see you later."

"Later, Gavin."

I slowly walked over to an area of the roof where there weren't too many people. I stood there for a while, sweating profusely, watching the evacuation process unfold. I looked straight across from where I was standing and I couldn't believe my eyes.

There was an elderly lady holding a poster board-sized sign against a tinted window that read, "HELP!"

I thought I was seeing things, so I rubbed my eyes and looked again. Sure enough "HELP!" was plastered to the window. I started to wave at the window for a few seconds when she finally put the sign down. I tried to yell to her, but she couldn't hear me. I made a signal so as to say, "Wait a second, I'll be right back," and ran back over to where Robert was, but he wasn't there. I asked one of the deputies, and he said he thought he went down to the second floor.

I went down there and after about five minutes of looking for him, I found him in one of his father-in-law's offices. "Hey Robert, there's an older woman on the top floor of the Municipal Court building holding a sign in the window that says, 'Help!'"

He stood up and said, "What? Where?"

I insisted, "Follow me, I think you can see her from the window over by my stuff."

We walked together and when we got there, sure enough, we could see her holding her sign.

"How long has she been there?" Robert asked.

"I have no idea," I told him. "I just saw her a few minutes ago when I was on the roof. Can you do anything for her?"

"I'm going to go find a radio and let someone know she's in there."

A few other people stood near us, looking at her. Periodically, she would put the sign down and wave to us again. As Robert walked off, a few of us made gestures to the lady; trying to encourage her. Since the window was solid and not broken that was all we could really do to communicate with her. It looked like she smiled and acknowledged us. I couldn't tell if she was by herself or not. We tried to get her to give us any indication if she was alone or not, but were unsuccessful in our attempts.

The few people standing around started to trickle off and, eventually, so did I. My dad was sitting down watching two little kids hitting each other, pushing each other, and just horsing around. "One of those kids is gonna get hurt," my dad told me. Not even five seconds later one of the kids fell backward and hit his head against the metal cabinet. Of course, he started crying.

Either the boy's mom or aunt, I guess, started hitting the other kid really hard and told him, "You stupid little #!*?" We sat there watching this unfold, and I really felt sorry for both of the kids.

My dad turned to me and whispered, "Damn, she's hitting the heck out of that kid'; she's gonna hurt him."

I shook my head in agreement and whispered back, "I'm glad you never did that to me; mom was a little rough with me, but not you."

"Well, Son, I never really believed in hitting a child."

"Yeah, Dad, I remember you shaking me when you were mad at me, but mom wouldn't hesitate to whack me a couple of times."

Half smiling at me he said, "You could be a handful when you were a kid, Son."

"Yeah, I probably did deserve a whack or two."

Shaking his head, my dad said, "Naw, Son, I learned a long time ago that spanking a child rarely did any good. Speaking of your mother, where is she anyway?"

"I honestly don't have a clue, Dad. I'm pretty sure she told me she was working on the train to Chicago. I think she told me she was leaving on Saturday or Sunday. I haven't spoken to her since last week some time."

"I hope she left the city."

"Me too, Dad. Me too."

We sat there for a few minutes watching the one kid crying and the other kid crying from the beating and scolding he took. The kid who had hit his head looked fine. It appeared he was crying more out of a need for attention than from pain. The other boy was sitting by himself crying, looking at the woman every once in a while.

All of the sudden, my dad said, "You know you shouldn't hit that kid like that! You're gonna — "

The woman turned her head and yelled, "Don't tell me how to handle my child!"

Instantly, I felt like this might be trouble. My dad stammered, "Hold up lady ... I'm not telling you how to ..."

"Listen, mind your own business old man!"

At this point I stood up, holding my hand up and pointing at my dad to be quiet. I said, "Hey, hey, he didn't mean any harm lady. We're sorry." She kind of gave a defiant look and turned back to talk to her sister or cousin or whomever she was talking to before the little kid took his beating.

That's part of the problem with some kids and parents in New

Orleans — they've lost their way. No one can tell anyone anything without them getting indignant, even when a good word would be helpful.

I sat back down next to my dad and whispered, "Dad, we know she shouldn't hit her kid that hard, but let's keep our comments to ourselves. We don't need anymore problems."

He scooted back on his mattress and lamented, "Yeah ... Okay, Son."

Not even 10 seconds later, some loud screaming and arguing came from behind us in the adjacent room. A high-pitched female voice said something to the effect of, "You ain't gonna tell me what to mutha' fuckin' do! You ain't my daddy!"

A booming male voice yelled, "Fuck you bitch! I'll knock your ass out!"

She countered with, "I ain't scared of your punk ass! Fuck you! Come on mutha' fuck ..."

This couple's gonna come to blows in a minute.

My dad said, "What the hell is all that about?"

"I don't know, but it doesn't sound good."

A few seconds later, the female, whom I now realized was the medical clerk who works on the 10th floor, walked through the doorway with her one-year-old son in her arms shouting, "You ain't gonna fuck with me! You bitch ass nigger! You fuckin' with the wrong one!"

Later I found out the man she was arguing with was just

somebody who had set up near them, and they were arguing about the space between them when the man began to threaten her.

I knew we were on the verge of everyone cracking. The heat was starting to affect everyone, and tempers were continuing to flare.

I decided to grab my book, the latest *Harry Potter*, to try to pass the time by reading. It was getting late, and I wasn't too confident we would be leaving that day. They were still evacuating the inmates to the Broad Street Bridge and then to buses below the bridges. I grabbed a nearby chair and moved it close to the shattered window and began to read. I only had about a 100 pages left, and I figured I would read until it got close to dusk. My dad laid back and turned his face toward the wall. I put the book down for a minute, grabbed my pillows, and fanned him until he fell asleep.

Once he was snoring again, I sat back down and read. I tried to engross myself in the book so I could escape the horrendous predicament I was in. I kind of lost track of time and eventually went to sleep too.

I woke up later with the book lying in my lap. I looked at my dad and all I could see was the right side of his face and body. It didn't look like he was breathing. I got that nervous feeling in my chest again and watched his face for what seemed like an eternity. Again, just when panic set in, he took a deep snoring breath through his nose and momentarily opened his eyes real wide, with his cheek quivering. He reached up and scratched his head and saw me looking at him. "What's wrong? Why are you looking at me?"

Relieved and startled at the same time, I said, "Oh, um ... I thought for a second that you had stopped breathing."

Half awake he said, "What? Why did you think that?"

"I've noticed over the past couple of days, when you're sleeping, sometimes you go a long time without breathing, and I thought that you had stopped breathing. Just as I was going to check your pulse or something, you took a deep snore through your nose and woke up."

He looked at me for a second or two and said, "I didn't know I did that."

"How could you? You're sleeping."

Chuckling, he said, "I guess you're right, Son. I'm all right though." With that, I got up and grabbed my water bottle and took a swig.

Evening was upon us, and there was no indication we would be leaving. It looked like another sweltering night in this cesspool. With the prospect of another night in there, I encouraged my dad to drink as much water as he could. I also suggested we prepare the MRE we had. "Hey Dad, are you hungry? We can fix this lasagna pack thing here, whatever it is."

"Yeah, I guess I could try it."

When I opened it up, I saw the directions on how to heat the lasagna. I have to say this was pretty neat. First, I took out the lasagna plate and then took the box and placed it on a flat surface (the floor). Then there were those black packets that looked like gun powder or black sand I placed under the lasagna plate, which, when a small amount of water is put in the packets, activates the black powder instantly, producing steam and making the water boil. Next, we folded the outer edges of the box over the lasagna plate and let it "cook" for 12 to 14 minutes.

How would military people have 14 minutes to wait for the food to heat if they were engaged in some sort of battle — or was this a civilian type of MRE just for a situation like ours?

My dad and I watched the steam coming from the side and top of this box. After a couple of minutes, we had a few people standing by us watching this meal percolate.

"How long it takes to cook?" came from my left.

"About 12 to 14 minutes according to the directions," I answered.

Someone else was asking me about the meal preparation. "Is that steam? Where's that coming from?"

I grabbed the top portion of the box and showed them the directions. "Just follow the directions right here. It's real easy."

Looking at the box for a second with a tinge of confusion on his face he said, "Oh, thanks man. Let me go and try that."

By this time, our meal was ready. Because of the heat, I wasn't really hungry, but I knew I had better eat something.

"Ready to eat, Pops?"

"Yeah, do we have to use our hands or what?"

"No, there's a fork here with the MRE for you to use. Here

you go. Enjoy!"

The food was still pretty hot and his first bite nearly fell out of his mouth. A few seconds later I said, "I bet you never thought you'd be eating military lasagna sitting on the floor of a jail, in your underwear, huh, Dad?"

With his mouth half full, he said, "Nope. Can't say that I did."

"Is it good?"

"Not bad, Son; here, try some." He handed me his fork and I took a bite. Surprisingly, it really wasn't too bad. I took another bite or two, and gave the fork back to my dad. "Finish it off, Dad; I'll eat a little later."

"You sure?"

"Go ahead." I wanted him to eat more, because it was obvious the bathroom was back to its nasty condition, and I didn't want to deal with that any more than I had to.

"You don't have any more M&Ms, do you?"

"No, I gave them to you earlier, but I'll see if I can trade something with somebody for some more M&Ms."

"Thanks."

"Hey, Dad, I'll be back in a minute. I'm going to go see if I can find anything out about when we'll be leaving here."

He casually replied, "See you later."

When I got to the roof, the sun was beginning to creep down toward the horizon. It was another beautiful day (except for the heat), without a cloud in the sky. The orange-blue sunset was becoming all too familiar. There were plenty of people on the roof, many of them getting prepared to sleep outside for the night. There were mattresses set up all over, and it would definitely be cooler at night up there than inside. I also think the smell of the building inside had gotten unbearable to most folks. If I had been by myself I would have been sleeping outside too.

After wandering around the roof for a while, I noticed the helicopter activity had slowed down, and I was hearing fewer boats moving around on the water. I didn't know if that meant there were fewer people to evacuate or because night was approaching, and with no lights in the city, they were going to shut it down for the night. I took one last look at the Broad Street Bridge, and there were still plenty of stranded civilians and a few inmates left. We might not be leaving that day, but we had to be getting close. Four days was enough. I looked over toward the Templeman Buildings and didn't see any inmates waving white sheets or towels for help or sitting on the rooftops anymore. I asked one of the deputies if he heard any news on when or where we were going.

"Man, I don't know! Anywhere but here is fine with me."

I was about to go back downstairs when I almost ran into Robert at the entrance to the roof. I said, "Just who I was looking for. Robert, are we leaving tomorrow?"

"Gavin, I'm fairly confident we will, but you know, who knows?" He shrugged his shoulders. "Be prepared to leave though. I'm still pretty sure we're going to move the elderly and sick first.

Remember, you can only bring one bag, if they let you take anything at all, that is."

"Yeah, I remember. See you later."

Back on the second floor, the scene was familiar. People of all walks of life lumped together, worn out, overheated, sitting or lying down, sleeping or dazed, listening to the few remaining radios with working batteries. It was getting dark inside and when I got over to my dad, I noticed someone had lit the candle. My dad was lying down with his hands behind his head just looking up at the ceiling.

"Hey, Dad, it looks like tomorrow."

Not even looking at me and with a sarcastic tone he said, "I'll believe it when I see it."

"Me too, but I heard that they're going to move the elderly and sick people first."

Defiantly, he replied, "Well, I'm not sick, Son, so that doesn't do us any good."

Laughing to myself I said, "Yeah, but you're elderly I know everyone thinks you're 50, but you technically fall under the elderly category."

"Yeah, but ..." He must have thought about it for a second and said, "Hey, whatever gets us outta here will work for me."

Smiling at him, I said, "Now you're thinking. Just go along with me, and we'll be outta here soon.'"

At that moment, someone was letting the bathroom door slam again: "BAM!"

"Damn door. I wish I had a dollar for every time that damn door slammed closed."

"I hear ya, Dad. I just wish when the door slammed the smell would get slammed out of the building."

"No kidding!" And we both laughed a little.

By this point, there wasn't much I could do on the 10th floor, but I knew I had to go up there for a little while, just in case something happened. I told my dad I would be back in a little while.

I could see the disappointed look on his face when I told him I'd be leaving.

"I guess I'll be here tonight — again."

I shook my head yes and said, "See you in a little bit," and began my way upstairs. I took one last look at him before I turned around. He was lying down, facing the wall again.

I got to the stairs and realized I didn't have my flashlight. I went to go back and took a few steps. *Ah, screw it.* I decided to walk the stairs in the dark. I figured by this point, all the inmates were evacuated, and there were no more wolf-dogs in the building. It took me several minutes to walk the stairs, and I imagined what it must be like to be blind.

Once I got to the 10th floor, covered in sweat, I couldn't believe how quiet and dark it was. No one was up there and everyone, including the inmates, was either on the roof, on the second floor, or evacuated. I decided since I was already on 10, I would try to make a phone call. After a couple of attempts with no success, I text-messaged Lora saying, "I LUV U. STILL HERE. HOPE 2 SEE U SOON. GAV." I got the confirmation it went through and took one last look outside, figuring it might be the last time I would do so. I didn't think I would be back. With all the rumored devastation to most of the building and the city, my time there was hopefully almost over. After contemplating for a few minutes, I made my way back downstairs, making a pit stop on the roof to see what was going on and to get one last bit of fresh air before going to my spot for the night.

The roof was bursting with people and activity. The word was spreading we'd be leaving in the morning, around 8 a.m. All the inmates from the entire system were evacuated with our building, HOD, being the last (of course). Although we were going to be the last ones evacuated, I could hear, for the first time, some optimism in everyone's voices.

"Are they really getting here?"

"Man, I thought they forgot about us!"

"I can't wait to get out of here!"

It seemed everyone on the roof had an opinion about when, where, and how we would be moved the next day.

I thought I would walk over to the side of the roof to see if the woman with the sign was still stranded. It was dark outside, except for the moon and billions of stars above, and a few flashlights shining about. I looked where I first saw her, but it was too dark to see anything. After a minute or two of straining my eyes to see anything,

I gave up and went back downstairs.

Maybe she'd gotten out safely.

Everyone on the second floor looked exhausted or was sleeping. The mood down there was not as animated as on the roof.

When I got near my dad he was talking to Dr. Marcus and Nurse Urban.

"What's up guys?" I asked.

My dad said, "Where you been, Son?"

Hesitating, I said, "I was on 10 for a few minutes and then on the roof for a little while — I have good news! We're supposed to be leaving in the morning around 8 a.m."

"Yeah, I heard that one before."

Dr. Marcus said, "Oh really? That's *great!*"

Urban said, "I really believe we will leave tomorrow ... I just don't know if it will be as early as they say."

For the next hour or so, we all sat around talking, sweating, sipping on water, still in disbelief we were in this horrible situation. Our little candle was lit, giving off the comforting light. As the conversations slowed down, I found myself lying back, peacefully watching the candle flicker.

Unfortunately, our respite was short-lived. Nearby someone had a radio on, and the news was still the same. The looting and raging fires seemed to dominate the airwaves, along with the reports of dead bodies and the water still rising in the city.

After some thought, I just prayed in the direction of the candle for a variety of things. First and foremost, for my dad's safety and health. As I prayed, the candle seemed to get brighter, and I got chills again — yes, real chills — down my entire body. In the midst of all this chaos and suffering, I really began to feel like maybe we were going to be all right.

I decided to get up and grab my pillow to fan my dad so he could go to sleep. The sooner he fell asleep, the sooner tomorrow would come, and hopefully we would be out of there. When he gave out a little snore every 10 seconds or so, I knew he was okay. It took me a while to fall asleep; well, I really never was completely at rest because I kept catching myself checking on him to make sure he was still breathing.

The last time I looked at my phone, it was around midnight. I decided at that point to turn it off to save the battery, because there was no way to charge it. I was only awake from pure adrenaline. My body was exhausted, but my mind was still racing.

Would we get out of here soon? Where would we live? Where would I work? I don't have a car. My dad's car is gone. What will I do with my dad? Where's my mom? Is my little brother alive?

On and on my mind kept racing with questions. I felt like I had it together, but still, I worried myself to sleep.

Chapter Eight

POP-POP-POP, POW, POW, POW!!

MORE GUNFIRE WOKE ME UP. A hint of daylight shone through the window, but no one else was awake. I looked over at my father and right on cue he gave a little snore. I was completely soaked in sweat. Going on my fifth day without a shower (if you don't count that ice cold, one-minute shower I took late Sunday night), my body odor was really starting to be noticeable. I started having daydreams of taking a two-hour bubble bath with my honey massaging my back and feeding me chocolate-covered strawberries or something.

Back to my reality: I grabbed my towel, which by then was pretty smelly too, and a little water and wiped myself down. I was starving and felt pretty weak, and I took a couple bites of a granola bar.

Lying back down, I noticed how hauntingly quiet it was inside and out. For the past couple days, the helicopters and flat boats had filled the air with loud whirring sounds, making it seem like a war zone. Imagining a better place to be, I must have fallen asleep again.

The next thing I knew, my dad was nudging me and whispering, "Gavin... Son... I gotta go to the bathroom." Same story, different day.

Once we finished, I changed into the last clean shirt I had and put on some shorts. It was sizzling hot already, but I didn't want to walk around in my underwear. I gave my dad one of my not-too-dirty T-shirts, so he could wipe the sweat off himself.

"Well, Son, I hope this is the day!"

Feeling optimistic, I exclaimed, "Me too, Dad! Hopefully, this morning sometime. Just be ready."

I got up and made my way to the roof. It was another beautiful clear day, and only a few people milled around. Some were talking while others were sitting under the ledge out of the sun. I saw Nurse Robert standing by the entrance to the parking garage looking out over the ledge.

Making my way over to him, I overheard someone say, "They were supposed to be here by 8 a.m. Where are they?"

I asked someone standing nearby what the time was and they said it was 8:20.

Damn! I don't see any signs of boats.

I made my way over to Robert and asked, "What's up?"

With a somewhat guilty look on his face he said, "I don't know. They were supposed to be here by 8 o'clock, and I don't see them anywhere."

"Who's they?"

"The D. O. C., I was told. Fuckin' I don't know. All I can tell you is that they know we're here, and somebody's gonna come and get us. Just be ready!" I could see he had probably been asked the same questions a thousand times.

Dejected, I took my time walking back downstairs. I decided not to say anything to my dad or for that matter to anyone else. It was only about 8:45. I saw a few nurses standing in the main hallway and stopped by them to chat for a little while.

Nurse Favis and Nurse Tech Michelle were leaning against the wall talking. "Can y'all believe this? It's Friday and we're still here," I said.

"We gotta get outta here soon. This is unbearable," Favis said.

"How's your dad? Is he all right?" Michelle asked.

"Okay, as far as I can tell. Thanks for asking. By the way, how is your finger? Does it still hurt?"

"It's real stiff and a pretty sore, but not too bad."

"Keep takin' those antibiotics and you should be all right. If I hear anything about leavin', I'll let y'all know," I said as I walked away.

It was after 9 a.m., and I still didn't hear sounds of boats. I did hear an occasional helicopter flying around the area though. I found my dad lying down, fanning himself with my pillow.

"What's up, Dad?"

"My blood pressure, I'm sure. I have one pill left ... are we going home soon or what?"

After all of this time I thought I had made it clear that going home was not an option. Did he really think we were going home? I waited a few seconds before I said anything. Going on a hunch and a prayer I said, "We're being moved out of here first, to dry land, and then we'll have to see about home. I know my house is flooded, and we can't go there. I don't know about your house yet. Let's just concentrate on getting outta here first."

He didn't say anything and neither did I. I didn't want to upset him. I felt like a broken record and wasn't quite sure where my dad's physical and mental state was.

The time was passing painfully slowly now and with the heat everyone was in slow motion. Nine a.m. became 10 and 10 became 11. I was really hungry, but I forced myself not to eat. I decided to take a walk toward the main hallway, near the exit to the inmate's recreational area. I was walking slowly with my head down when all of the sudden Robert came through the second-floor stairwell door yelling, "Sick and elderly people, let's go! There are some boats ready to go! Sick and elderly people, let's …"

As I turned around, Robert walked fast toward me and said, "Get your bag and your dad and get to the roof. Now! Hurry!"

Caught by surprise, I ran back over to my dad and said, "Put your shoes, socks, and pants on — we're outta here!" He was lying down and half out of it. "Come on, Dad, we're leaving!"

"Are we going home?"

"Dad, get up and get dressed. We have to go to the roof now!"

Helping him get his stuff together, I put on my socks and tennis shoes and zipped up both bags. Since I had stuffed them full they were heavy. I helped him stand up and get his balance. For the first time in a while we both smiled at each other, knowing that we were getting out of there. "Come on, Dad, I'll carry both bags! Your left shoe is untied. Tie it real quick!"

The stairwell was still quite dark. I had a bag on each shoulder and told him to hold the handrail and the bag on my right shoulder. "Follow me slowly up the stairs. We only have to go one and a half flights of stairs, and then we'll go through a door that will lead to the roof!"

Confused, he said, "Why are we going to the roof?"

"Just follow me. You'll see!"

Once we were on the roof, there were about 10 or 12 people with us who fell under the sick and elderly category. Nurse Donna was with her husband (who recently had to retire due to poor health); Deputy Harriet and her uncle, who had a history of strokes and needed help walking; Ms. Cece, a rank official, had her mother who needed to be moved, as she needed dialysis.

The individual who needed medical attention most urgently was Deputy Lee. He was a tall black man in his mid- to late-30s who had diabetes and had injured his big toe during the aftermath. He had gone a few days without his insulin, and his feet were starting to swell, causing him to walk with an obvious limp. I asked, "What happened?"

He looked at me grimacing and said, "Man, I don't even remember. All I know is that the pain in my foot is killing me!" As we all stood by the doorway that led us one step closer to freedom, I saw Captain Brumfield and asked him how bad the building was.

"Well G, I don't see us back here for a long time — at least a year. Half of those buildings have holes in the walls where the inmates tried to escape. All the Templeman buildings are probably destroyed. CCC is real fucked up too. Don't worry about comin' back here any time soon. It's been nice workin' with ya, G — good luck!"

Shaking his hand I said, "All right, Cap, take it easy. Good luck!" I stood there for a minute, realizing that my time there was finally ending, but it was the first time I realized for exactly how long. My feelings were foggy. Relief. Sadness. Confusion. They called to us to walk through the doorway.

We made our way to the parking garage that connected to the roof and down the ramp to the bottom level. The water was a good way up the bottom level ramp, at least seven to eight feet or so. There were two flat boats and another boat. Once we got to the bottom level, we filed into each boat. There were three or four deputies helping those who needed it. Each boat was surrounded by all kinds of debris — sticks, trash, paper, a couple tires — just about anything I could think of. Everyone was trying to get on the boats too fast, frustrating the individuals navigating the boats.

"We're going to have to make a couple of trips, so everyone just be patient."

I had my dad sit down on the curb that ran up the driveway. "Let's just wait for the second trip. The bridge isn't that far away, and there's no use in hurrying up now. We'll just be on that bridge in the heat anyway."

"That's fine, Son. At least we're sort of moving."

People stepped up on a little piece of concrete sticking up out of the water to get into the boats. The only problem was one of the boats was much higher than the other. I noticed a strong gasoline smell.

One of the deputies said, "All those motorcycles and cars up there were being siphoned off for gas — that's what they've been running the boats off of." Looking up, I saw a row of police motorcycles and cars. Thank God those vehicles were there, because they were the only source of gasoline available.

After about 15 minutes, one of the boats came back. It was a different-looking boat. It pulled up as close as it could, and a man yelled to us, "Let's go! You two!"

I grabbed both bags and my dad got up, losing his balance a little. We got as close as we could to the boat without stepping into the water. Deputy Stan, a tall, strapping young African-American, was standing in the water with boots on. He and I worked on the 10th floor from time to time, and he kept order up there better than any other deputy. Stan turned to my dad and said, "Come on, Pops, I got ya." With that, he stepped toward my dad and picked him up like he was a bag of groceries, and put him in the boat. It was funny to watch because my dad is a pretty tall man. I tossed each bag on the boat, stepped on the section of cement and got in. My feet got wet and I had thoughts of contamination covering them.

As I positioned myself in the front of the boat, we backed up out of the garage and went down the street navigating carefully around the cars and trash in the water. The Broad Street Bridge was about 200 yards away, and as we approached the bridge we pulled up right next to the circular on-ramp. I threw the bags over the guardrail, stepped up on and then over the rail and onto the concrete on-ramp. My dad stepped across the boat on the edge, and I grabbed him under his arm while the man in the boat pushed him up and I pulled him over the guardrail. We slowly walked up the ramp on to the upslope of the bridge. "Well, we're out of there, thank God!" I could see my dad was a little disoriented and really didn't know what to say.

We walked over to where the others were and sat down. It was hot as hell, and the sun felt like it was beating down directly on us. The deputy with the bad toe had his shoe off looking at his foot. I walked over to him and right away noticed his big toe was split on the outside below the nail, but there was no blood. It was also quite swollen and greenish in color. He looked at me and said, "Whatcha' think, Doc? This sonofabitch is hurtin' real bad." When I looked at it, I instantly knew that it didn't look good. It appeared to have gangrene and needed immediate medical attention. He might well lose that toe.

"Man, you need to get medical assistance ASAP. Try to stay off of that foot as much as possible."

He looked away and then back at me and said, "Am I gonna lose my toe or what?"

Trying to stay positive, I said, "I don't know. Do you know

where we are going from here? If you can get medical attention soon, I think it will be all right."

"Hey, I stepped in a lot of that dirty water ... you think it'll be okay?" I figured the toxic water probably contributed to his condition.

"I don't know man. Let me get a bottle of water and we'll clean it off."

I went over to one of my bags and got a fresh, unopened bottle of water and one of my T-shirts. I poured the water over his toe and tried to clean it as best as I could while he clenched his teeth in pain. I finished cleaning his toe and gave him my T-shirt to wrap around his foot. Meanwhile, my dad was starting to wander up the bridge, and there were a lot of rough-looking characters walking around near him. I didn't want him to get into any trouble, so I yelled, "Hey Dad, come here!" He turned around, and I waved him toward me. A military helicopter flew over us and circled around, landing in the middle of the bridge. We were sitting about 100 yards or so from where the helicopter landed, and the wind generated from the propellers was furious.

Everyone around us started talking saying, "Are we supposed to be getting on the helicopter or what?" In the opposite direction, we were surrounded by water and in the distance down Broad Street, some boats headed our way. No one told us anything when we were evacuating the House of Detention building, and we had no idea what to do or where we were going. It was beyond frustrating.

I told my dad to sit down next to Deputy Lee. "I'm gonna go up to the top of the bridge to see if I can find out where the heck we're going." I got up and walked quickly to the top of the bridge. There were maybe about 200 people, predominantly black, elderly, and most looked somewhat ill.

The dismay and desperation on everyone's faces will always be burned in my memory.

At the top of the bridge was a rope tied from one side of the bridge to the other. There were about three or four black men ranging from about 16 years of age to about 40. They were directing people toward the helicopter that had just landed on the bridge and helping those people get into the chopper. I eventually got one of them to come over to me so I could ask them where the helicopters were going, if we were to get on them, whether we should get on the boats, things like that. The helicopter was just taking off stirring up a tremendous amount of wind, dust and trash. I yelled, "Do you know where we're supposed to go?!"

Squinting his eyes from the wind, he yelled back, "To the airport; sick first, then the elderly!" He then pointed to an area across from me to my left saying, "There is the line! You got any sick or old people with you?"

I turned around and pointed to our group at the bottom of the bridge and said, "Yes! Some sick; one real bad. And some elderly!"

The man pointed again to the line and said, "Get in line!"

As I walked back down the bridge, I saw an abandoned car casting some shade to its side. I decided to go get my dad and let him lie down on my bag in the shade so he wouldn't overheat.

When I got down to everybody, I said, "The helicopters are going to the airport, bringing sick and elderly first. We have to get in line and as the helicopters land, we'll be directed to get on them."

Donna said, "What about the boats? Where are they going?"

Realizing I didn't think to ask about the boats, I said, "It was so loud I didn't even ask. I figured the airport wouldn't be that bad, and they were getting the sick and elderly off the bridge first."

Deputy Lee started to stand up and lost his balance a little, so I helped him up. As he gained his balance, with great determination he said, "I'm going to get in that line. I gotta get my toe looked at as soon as possible."

As the group started to talk about what to do, I walked my dad over to the abandoned car and said, "Sit here, out of the sun until we can get on one of those helicopters."

"Where are they going to bring us? Home?"

Agitated and saddened by my dad's denial of the situation, I said, "Dad, we don't have a home to go home to. The helicopters are bringing people to the airport. Sick and elderly people first."

He nervously asked, "You're gonna be with me, right?"

"Of course, Dad. We're in this together until it's over." I had to force back tears.

I went back up toward the top of the bridge to watch for another helicopter. The men directing the people on the bridge formed another line for "immediate needs" individuals and as I heard them talking, I ran back down to gather everybody up. "Hey y'all, they're making another line for immediate needs individuals to fly out to the airport. Let's get in line!"

Everybody stood up, some faster than others, and began to walk up the bridge. Deputy Harriet's uncle was having a hard time, so I grabbed his bag for him. I was now walking up the bridge with three bags, one on each shoulder and one in my hands, like an overloaded hotel bellman or something.

Once we got to the top of the bridge, there wasn't much organization, and I could see people were going to be aggressive in their attempts to get on the helicopters. The next one was in the process of landing as we sat down in line. One of the "guys in charge" was a young, African-American kid about 16 or 17 years old with no shirt on and his shorts hanging halfway off his butt. "All right, ya'll, listen up! I'll wave y'all forward when the chopper lands ... only two or three at a time. Keep ya heads down, ya heard me?"

This is unbelievable. We have a teenager directing a military evacuation after a major disaster. No one would believe me if I told them this!

I helped Deputy Lee with his stuff to the front of the line yelling, "I am a nurse, and this man needs to get out of here! On this chopper! He needs immediate medical attention or he will lose his toe!"

"All right. All right. When they give me the signal, he can go!" A deputy and I looked at each other and sniggered for a second. I'm sure he was thinking the same thing I was thinking, *Look at this kid running the show! Unbelievable!*

After a minute or so, the military person in the helicopter made a hand gesture and our "leader" motioned for Deputy Lee to come forward. I grabbed his bag and helped him to the chopper, fighting the hurricane-force wind from the blades. Once he was safely in, I went back by my dad, barely keeping my balance and standing over him, covering his face to protect him from all the trash and dust flying all over the place. A couple people from our group got on the helicopter along with a few other people who needed immediate attention. I yelled to my dad, "We'll wait for the next one, okay?"

He nodded in agreement, and I kept protecting his face until the helicopter flew off.

About five minutes later, another chopper landed on the bridge, and this time it was rushed by a crowd of people. It was becoming a dog-eat-dog situation. I told my dad we would wait for a couple more helicopters, since they seemed to be coming with regularity. "There's no use in fighting the crowd right now. We're in line to get out of here before a lot of these people who have been on this bridge longer than us."

At this point I could see he was worn out. We both were. I approached Deputy Harriet and her uncle and suggested we stick together and I would help her with her uncle. "That's fine, Gavin. We'll go when y'all go."

There were about eight of us left, and I stood up and said,

"We'll catch one of the next couple of helicopters." Everyone nodded in agreement. I went to one of the guys directing traffic and said, "Our group right here will try and all get on together. We have a few people who need medical attention, but nothing that is an emergency."

"All right, bra' (brother). We'll try for the next one," he said. We nodded thank you.

About 10 minutes later, another chopper landed and we got up together and waited for the signal. I grabbed our bags and Deputy Harriet's uncle's bag. I put my hand on top of my dad's head and told him, "Keep your head down as we approach the helicopter!"

We ambled purposefully as the wind from the blades nearly knocked us down. I threw the bags in the helicopter toward an empty seat in the back, then helped my dad step up on to the floorboard to the last empty seat. Then I helped Harriet's uncle on to the floor of the helicopter, and I sat on the floor right in front of my dad. All the while, the noise from the chopper blades was deafening.

There was a seatbelt that came down over both of my dad's shoulders and hooked into a center buckle that came from under the seat. There was also a circular buckle that locked from both sides. I could see my dad was struggling with figuring out how it worked. I halfway turned around and hooked it together for him.

He smiled and I yelled, "We're finally out of this nightmare!"

The entire floor of the helicopter was filled with maybe 15 to 20 people mostly sitting on the floor. Everyone had a nervous look on his or her faces.

There were two military guys in the front and another guy in the back with us. They all had helmets and sunglasses on and looked quite intimidating, but were very friendly. Those guys were the best. The one in the back with us made a hand gesture to the pilot and then to the guys on the ground as they backed up from the helicopter. About 10 seconds later, we started to lift off the ground, and I got that "tickling butterflies" sensation in my stomach that I'd only had on a roller coaster before. My dad was smiling, so I guess he was feeling the same sensation I was. We went straight up, then dipped down and started to fly north, toward Lake Pontchartrain. In my 33 years of existence, I had never been on a helicopter, and this ride was truly amazing. I'm not quite sure what type of helicopter it was, but it was black, fast, and modern-looking. It may have been a Blackhawk or something close to it.

Flying toward the lake, I looked out to my right, and I could see that the entire area right off of the I-10 Interstate (the highway included) was completely under water. We veered to the left, and I could see where the levee had broken at the Seventeenth Street Canal. What a sight. A fateful, dreadful sight.

The next second I looked to my left and there was no floodwater anywhere. It was very strange to see all that water to the east side of the canal, but no water to the west. It appeared the Metairie side of the canal didn't break. All I saw was house after house with roof damage, trees down everywhere, signs scattered all over the streets, cars strewn everywhere, but no signs of people anywhere. Strange, strange and ghostly, actually.

It dawned on me we were flying in the direction of my home in Kenner, so I waited a few seconds, and I tried to look toward where I lived. As far as I could tell the flooding was down or gone. I couldn't see my condominium, but the destruction in the area was quite evident. Soon we turned and started our descent to the airport.

I could see people unloading from numerous helicopters, all in a line by a long runway strip. As we landed, I saw the vehicles airlines use to move luggage on to planes. We landed just about how we took off and rolled up in a perfect line behind a number of other helicopters. It was a 10-minute flight I will never forget, and I'm sure my dad won't either.

As I went to step off of the helicopter, I nearly fell down because I had no feeling in my right foot. I guess someone had been sitting on it. After helping Deputy Harriet's uncle and a few others down, I jumped back up into the chopper and helped my dad get unhooked and off the helicopter. Waiting for us was one of the luggage vehicles. We were directed to sit on the side of one of them.

I threw our bags in the middle, helped my dad up on to the side, and hopped in.

A wave of emotions hit me when we started to move, and tears welled up in my eyes. The reality we were finally out of that nightmare situation and on dry land coupled with the fact my dad was still alive hit me hard. Real hard.

Prisoners of Katrina

What is next?

When we went toward the main area of the airport, I could see what looked like hundreds of people standing, sitting, or walking around. The odd thing was it looked like most people could hardly move. A few minutes or so later we pulled up to an unloading area near a gate, and all I saw was a turbulent sea of people – all kinds of harried people. On one side, I saw an area that looked like a M.A.S.H. medical unit.

We were told to go through an open gate, and as we started to walk, an elderly man with a walker shuffling along started to fall.

I gave one of the bags to my dad and helped this old man slowly walk through the gate and over to the makeshift medical area. My dad walked straight ahead through the gate and sat down on the curb under the down-ramp of the second level of the airport. This appeared to be an area where most of the people were going. A military medical person met me at the entrance to the medical unit.

"What is his medical problem?"

"I don't know sir; I was just helping him walk from the drop-off area." The elderly man stood silent with his head bowed.

"I'll take it from here. Thanks."

I walked over and sat down by my dad. Exhausted and relieved, I said, "Well, Buddy, at least we're on dry land and out of the city!"

My dad looked at me and asked, "Now what?"

I just looked around at the crowd of people wandering around. Just about everyone looked disoriented or confused. I asked my dad to sit down and said I would walk around to see if anyone knew what was going on. As I stood up, I saw a gigantic African-American man struggling to walk through the gate leading to where we were.

The man was in obvious pain.

There were people walking right by him, not offering any help. I stood there for a few seconds and watched him try to walk. He wore what looked like work boots, shorts, and a torn T-shirt. He was well over 300 pounds and well over 6 feet tall. Once I realized no one was with him or was going to help him, I went over and offered, "Hey Buddy, you need some help?" He looked surprised someone was willing to help him.

"Well, Yes. Thanks. Thank you, Son." I could see his legs were swollen and his feet were in immense pain by the way he was walking. I asked him, "What's wrong with your feet?" With what looked like all the energy he had left, he said, "I have diabetes, and my feet have sores on them. I haven't had my medicine in a few days." I figured he probably had foot ulcers.

Trying to reassure him, I said, "Well, sir, they have some sort of medical area set up over there. If you want, I can help you over there to see if they can help you."

"Man, I would appreciate that."

I got on the left side of this gargantuan man and put my right arm around his waist and told him to lean on my right shoulder and try to walk. It took us an agonizingly long time to walk about 50 yards to the medical area. When we finally reached it, I shouted,

"This man is a diabetic and needs immediate medical attention!" One of the nurses turned around and ran toward an area where they had transport vehicles and the other nurse or doctor said, "We got him."

The man turned to me and shook my hand saying, "Thanks man. Thank you." His eyes reddened with gratitude.

Smiling, I said, "You're welcome. Good luck, man."

I looked to my left and saw the deputy with the bad toe being helped through a doorway on the side of the main building. I hoped he'd be all right.

I walked toward the main doorway to the bottom level of the airport. There were people lying on the ground, sitting against the wall, walking around, talking, arguing, eating, sleeping — anything imaginable. I went further and all I saw were more people and more calamity. I walked up to someone who looked like they might work there and said, "Can you tell me what to do or where to go?" The guy looked agitated and pointed up toward the escalators and stairs that were filled with people. I stood there for a second, looking at everyone fighting their way to get up the stairs and decided to wait a little while and go up there later.

I went back over by my dad and saw him buying some cigarettes from a drunk-looking guy. I was going to say something, but decided not to. I could see the stress on my dad's face, so I figured if he thought he needed a cigarette, he should have one. I sat back down next to him, and we had our group together from the HOD. There was an area right next to the medical area where some people were putting bottles and bottles of water into a huge "pool looking" structure filled with ice behind a loose chain-link fence. I immediately got up, pointed and told everyone, "Hey, look, they're giving out water over there. Let's get some!" A few of us walked over there and grabbed some bottles of water. Word spread fast and mobs of people started attacking the bottled water pool. We got ours and got out of the way. Those in charge realized they had to create some order, so they closed the chain-link gate and started handing water over the fence to people who needed or asked for it.

Of course, there were people taking advantage and getting more than they needed.

About 15 minutes later, a forklift came from out of nowhere with a crate full of MREs. A couple of military individuals stood by us as the crate was lowered to the ground and MREs were handed out. I got in line and got one each for my dad and me. This would be our first full meal in a few days. I went back over to the curb and ripped open the MRE to see what I could eat. I gobbled up a bag of trail mix real quick. My main meal was a vegetarian one and my dad's was beef with mushrooms.

I don't know if I was super hungry or what, but the MRE tasted like filet mignon to me! As we ate, the guy my dad bought the cigarettes from was lying face down on the concrete passed out. All of a sudden, he started coughing and jerking around a little. He then started dry heaving and about 30 seconds later started vomiting. He was obviously drunk or on some kind of illicit drugs. He woke up and stood up while everybody in the immediate area jumped up and got out of his way. He looked around for a few seconds and said, in an impaired manner, "I'm all right, yeah, yeah, I'm good!" while wiping the puke from his face. Everyone watching started to giggle a bit as the man staggered around and wandered off.

Due to the smelly mess he made near us, we decided to slide down the curb a little way. I went over to where they were handing out water and poured a few bottles over the vomit to help wash it away. Once we got resettled, I finished eating, although it wasn't as appealing as it was before. I told our group I was going to go up to the upper level to see what our next move would be. I walked back over to the escalator and stairs area and maneuvered my way up. The upper level of the Louis Armstrong International Airport is where you go to check in for a flight, and it has all sorts of restaurants, shops, a video arcade, etc.; of course, all closed up. As I stepped off the last step to the second floor, I was stunned at what I saw: thousands and thousands of people packed together wandering about. I could barely walk forward from the top step and didn't know which way to go. I stepped to my right to get out of the way, but that was virtually impossible.

Frantically, people walked and ran into each other, crying and yelling in outright bedlam. I saw what looked like an airport employee and fought through the crowd toward him, getting bumped and knocked around in the process. Once I got to him, I yelled, "Do you know what we're supposed to do? I just got here a short time ago!"

It took this guy a second to catch his breath and then he said, as he pointed behind me, "You have to get in line over there to get registered to get on a plane to somewhere, either San Antonio, Austin, Dallas, somewhere like that!"

I turned around and my heart sank in my chest. There was a line that extended for as far as I could see filled with people crying, screaming, talking loudly, and yelling.

I turned back to the man and asked, "Is that the only way outta here?!"

Apologetically, he answered, "Yes! But from that line you have to get into that line to get on a plane, and you don't have a choice as to where you go. I've heard people will be on military bases for a month or so!"

Just as I turned back to ask the man something else, an older man fell over, hit the ground, and appeared to have a seizure. The man I was talking to instantly grabbed a walkie-talkie and said, "I need medical backup by the main escalator! Man down! I repeat – I need backup!"

At this point I didn't know what to do. By law, I am a nurse and if I initiate treatment on this guy I can become liable if something goes wrong, but I couldn't let this guy lie there and not do anything. His wife, I guess, started crying hysterically, so I told her to help me turn him on his side and she needed to hold him there until help came. I got down and turned the man on his side, making sure his head was parallel to the floor, and told the woman to hold him as steady as she could until help came. The lady frantically said, "Oh! Are you a doctor?"

"No ma'am. Just do it!" As I got up to walk away, she thanked me, and I didn't even look back. I walked toward the back of the first line, and it went on forever. I turned to look at the second line and saw it was worse. It was so loud and crowded I decided to go toward the sliding glass doors that led to the outside of the second level.

Pacing outside, I tried to compose myself, as I could feel anxiety and panic building. I tried to breathe slow, deep breaths. Looking left, I saw a convoy of military vehicles unloading people. To my right, I saw a row of yellow port-a-lets and a few armed military personnel guys directing traffic. Down toward the end, to the right, I saw a tall, broad-shouldered Caucasian army soldier with a gun, standing by himself. I decided to go over to him to see if he had any ideas as to what was going to happen.

I walked up to him and asked, "Have you ever seen anything like this before?"

He looked at me for a second, curled a smile, and said, "I was in Iraq for over a year, and I never saw anything close to this. This is unbelievable! This is something like out of a movie. It's crazy!"

I waited a second or two before I asked, "What should I do? I have my 83-year-old dad with me, and he's out of his medicine. They're saying inside we have to get on a plane and fly to Texas, but they don't know where."

He was half-joking and half-serious, I guess, when he replied,

"Man, if I were you I would go try and steal a car or something and drive the hell out of here!" He paused for a couple of seconds and then said, "The only problem is they might stop you a few miles down the road at the checkpoint to see if the car is yours." Smiling, he pointed and said, "Across the highway there (pointing to the south) I heard there are different police agencies; you might be able to find out something over there."

I stood there watching people unload from various military vehicles. I still didn't know what to do. I shook the guy's hand and thanked him. "Good luck," he said.

Another "good luck." Seemed to be a lot of those going around.

I shuffled back toward the sliding glass doors contemplating what to do. I did not want to get on some plane and go to a military base for who knew how long with my dad. Would we be under Marshal Law? What exactly did that mean? I couldn't see him making it through that scenario after all he'd been through so far.

I looked up and saw, once again — total chaos. I decided I couldn't and wouldn't board a plane. I had to figure something out fast.

Getting knocked around like a pinball, I made my way back to the escalator and stairway where I had come from. I didn't walk 30 feet before another person keeled over, falling into the person next to him. I wanted to stop and help, but I had to keep going, to get my dad and me out of there. This happened two more times before I could get off the second level down to the ground level. It was more and more surreal.

This can't be real! I must be dreaming!

Over near my dad and the others, I saw Deputy Rico and his family and a couple of nurses from the House of Detention building. They saw me and made their way over. "Hey Gavin. How long have you been here?"

Surprised to see them, I said, "Hey y'all! Not long, an hour or two. I'll tell you, though, this is as bad — if not worse — than where we were before! It's a freakin' mad house on the second level. They got people passing out, fighting to get in line! No one knows what the hell is goin' on!"

A few seconds later, some Louisiana State Police officers approached and asked Deputy Rico to show some identification because he had his firearm on his hip. Defensively, he said, "I'm an Orleans Parish deputy, and we just got here. I'm tryin' to find out what the hell is going on!"

One of the state officers then said, "You're gonna have to come with us and turn that gun in ... you can't walk around with it in this environment."

Turning back to me, he said, "Can you believe this shit? Do me a favor and tell my wife I'll be back in a minute!"

Shaking my head in disbelief, I said, "No problem. Don't worry, I'll tell 'em."

I saw his wife and kids about 50 yards away, but before I could get to them, Nurse Favis, her daughter, and Nurse Beatrice came up to me saying, "What's up G? We made it!"

I hastily said, "I don't know, this is pretty bad too. Have you been on the second level yet?"

They looked at each other and said, "Not yet ... why?" I proceeded to tell them about the frenzied scene up there and how if you get on a plane you would be flown to Texas somewhere with no definite plan.

"I ain't getting on no plane ... screw that!" Beatrice shouted. Favis stood there blankly.

"Go take a look for yourself. If you decide to get on a plane you better get in line now or there's no tellin' how long it will take to get outta here. Hey y'all, I'm going back over by my dad and the others so I can tell 'em what's going on." Pointing behind them toward the down ramp over the unruly crowd, I said, "I'll be over there until I figure out what to do. See y'all later."

As I walked back to my dad, all I saw were ailing people: people in wheelchairs, lying on tables with I.V. lines in their arms, and lying on the ground receiving medical care. I started to feel a slight bit better at the sight of this many people getting the medical care they needed.

I prayed silently my dad wouldn't end up in there.

Everyone in our area just looked dog-tired. Nurse Donna sipped on bottled water while wiping the sweat from her forehead as her husband leaned back on his bag, half asleep. My dad was standing up smoking a cigarette, still looking somewhat disoriented. Deputy

Harriet saw me and pulled me to the side saying, "Hey G, my uncle needs to go to the bathroom. Can you help me?"

Pointing up and behind us I said, "Yeah sure. The only bathrooms I saw were port-o-lets, outside on the second level." She looked at me with a frustrated look. I added, "Let's go over to that medical area. I'm sure with your uncle's condition (partial paralysis from a stroke) they will help you. They must have a useable bathroom in there."

We got him up and helped him walk over to the medical unit, and they did take him in. Deputy Harriet went in with him and as she went to go in, she thanked me. I could see she was really worried about him, and I was happy to help her.

In the rush to evacuate her family, Deputy Harriet told me after everyone had evacuated, she realized no one had remembered to get her uncle, so she had to get him and bring him to the prison. She said, "Thank God I went and got him, because he lives in Gentilly (eastern New Orleans, near the lake). He probably would have drowned!"

Once she was inside with him, I walked back over to our spot and sat down for a minute to take a break. I needed to think about what to do. My house was only a couple miles from the airport and although I was sure it was flooded, maybe the upstairs portion was all right, just maybe. Could we stay up there? My main concern was the fact there was no electricity there and it would be very hot. It was starting to seem more appealing to fly out of there.

I eventually stood to get everyone's attention, "Hey, everybody!" Gathering my composure, I said with as loud a voice as I could without screaming, "Basically, once you go to the second level, you have to get in a line to give your information to get on a plane. Once you get out of the first line, which is a mile long, you have to get in a second line, which is even longer. That puts you on a plane to somewhere in Texas either San Antonio, Austin, Dallas or somewhere like that. If you fly out of here, you will probably end up on a military base under marshal law for no tellin' how long!"

As soon as I stopped talking, obviously out of breath, everybody started yelling out expletives and complaints.

"Are you kidding me?"

"This is bullshit! I'm not gettin' on no plane!"

"Hell with that! What the …?"

As I sat back down and listened to all the desperation and frustration, I looked forward and saw a news camera pointing in our direction, filming all the commotion. When the cameraman turned, I could see it was CNN News. The reporter was starting to talk to people and he would occasionally look back toward the camera. They were documenting this historic event. Historic, sad, and deplorable.

My phone vibrated in my pocket. Grabbing it, I looked at the screen and it read, "WHERE R U? WHAT IS GOING ON? TEXT ME OR CALL ME. MISS U. LORA."

I sent a message saying, "AT AIRPORT. IT' S CRAZY HERE. MAY HAVE TO CATCH PLANE TO TEXAS. MISS U 2. WILL

TRY TO CALL. GAV." I pressed the send button and got the confirmation it was sent.

Turning toward my dad and Donna, I said, "I'm going to walk across Airline Highway toward my house to see how bad it is. We're (my dad and I) not getting on a plane unless we have no choice. I don't live too far from here, so I should be back in a couple of hours. Dad, stay here, don't wander off anywhere!"

I leaned over to Donna and whispered in her ear, "Please keep an eye on him." She winked at me and nodded her head in acknowledgement.

Disconcerted, my dad said, "I'm not gonna wander anywhere, Son."

Donna caught me, "Hey Gavin, my son doesn't live too far from here. About a mile. Go by his house and see if they're there. He said he wasn't leaving for the storm." I walked back over to her and gave her a piece of paper out of my wallet and told her to write the address and phone number down, just in case the phone worked.

After getting the information, I told them I'd see them in a couple of hours and I was off. It was after 4 p.m. now and still hot as could be. It didn't take five minutes of walking before I was covered in sweat. As I approached the Hilton Hotel across the highway from the airport, I could see there were all kinds of police and military personal walking in and out of the front door and was stopped by some sort of law officer. I didn't recognize his uniform, but he was obviously not going to let me in. Approaching him I said, "Hi, how ya doin'?"

He was a middle-aged white man who looked as tired as everyone else. He looked at me for a second or two and said, "Can I help you?"

Trying to be optimistic, I said, "I hope so. I just got evacuated from downtown to the airport and after asking around for a little while, I was told the only way out of the city was to get on a plane to Texas." I paused for a second and said, "I only live a couple of miles from here and wanted to go look at my house to see if it is livable."

Eyeing me up for a few seconds the man said, "You could try, but there are military road blocks set up all over the area. I doubt they will let you through, but you could try."

Pointing left and behind me, I asked, "How far down is the first road block?"

"Half a mile or so, I guess."

"All right, sir. Thanks for the info."

As I walked away, he said, "Wait a minute! There's another roadblock in the opposite direction about three miles down. I think if you can get someone to come get you they will let them through, providing proof they are here to get you."

Lora is in Texas. It would take at least eight hours for her to get me.

"Thanks again for the info, see ya later!"

"Good luck!"

I decided to walk toward the checkpoint in the direction of my house. It was closer to a mile than half a mile. At least it felt longer.

Nearing Williams Boulevard at Airline Highway, I saw two Hummer-looking vehicles with a few young National Guardsmen standing with guns directing various vehicles. There were also some state police in the area. I slowly walked up to one of those guys and asked, "Hi, how are you doing? I live (pointing to my left) a couple of miles from here. I just got evacuated from downtown and wanted to go see if my house is — "

Before I could finish my sentence he interrupted, "No, sorry. The area is on lock-down, and curfew will be starting soon. We're under Marshal Law!" I didn't even get to ask him anything else, as he just walked away from me. Aggravated, I walked off back toward the airport as the sun beat down on my sweaty, overheated body.

I started to feel as if my head was going to explode. I was getting very upset, anxious, overheated, and pissed off all at the same time. I started talking to myself, probably looking like a schizophrenic or something. A million thoughts collided in my mind. All of a sudden, I broke into an all-out sprint.

The next thing I know, I was leaning over trying to catch my breath. *What the hell am I doing?*

It took me about 20 minutes to get back to our spot.

Donna said, "Damn, that was quick!"

I'm sure I looked frustrated as I responded with, "They wouldn't let me go to my damn house! This is bullshit!"

Not even 30 seconds later I got a call that changed everything. Startled, I answered and was overjoyed to learn it was my friend,

Corey. He lives in Bayou Gauche, which is south of New Orleans about 30 miles from downtown and about 20 to 30 minutes from the airport. With his subtle Cajun accent, he said, "Hey bra', you alive?"

With a surge of adrenaline I said, "Dude, I'm alive! I'm at the New Orleans airport. I just got here a couple hours ago, and it's fuckin' crazy here. Where are you?"

"I'm at home. We just got back earlier today from Shreveport. Man, I saw the news and they showed your work and said there were riots and hostages and shit like dat!"

"Corey, listen! You gotta come get us from the airport! It's …"

"Who's us? Lora ain't with ya is she?"

"No, no! Me and my dad! His stubborn ass wouldn't leave so I got him to come down and stay with me at work. Big mistake."

I don't know exactly how he responded because as I was talking to him my phone started to beep and I saw it was from Lora's number. "Hey Corey, Hang on a second. Lora is trying to call me. If we get disconnected, call me back or text message me all right?"

Before I could hear his response, I clicked over and said, "Hey baby, am I glad to hear your voice!"

I could hear her starting to cry. "Are you okay?"

"Yes, Sweetie, I was just on the phone with Corey when you called. It was the first time my phone worked in a while. Did you get my text message?"

"Yeah, baby. I want to come get you, but they don't want me to!"

Stunned to hear her say that, I asked, "What? Who doesn't want you to?"

"Everybody. My family, your cousins ..."

Confused, I said, "My cousins? Who?"

"Scott and Craig. Baby, listen. It's crazy all over the state! The news is reporting people are stealing cars and when they run out of gas they are ramming other people's cars and stealing them! They're also saying gas is hard to get. Scott and Craig are worried something like that could happen to me." I listened to her and couldn't believe what I was hearing. It was anarchy.

Exasperated, I said, "They're tellin' us we have to get on a plane and go to Texas to military bases, and I'm not doin' that! Besides, my dad is out of his medicine ... I ... j -j-just ... damn ... shit man! Somebody's gotta come get us!"

I could hear her getting upset again saying, "Baby, what do you want me to do?"

She began to cry and I started to feel bad. "Hey, hey, I'm sorry. It's just insane down here. We gotta get outta here soon!"

Composing herself, she said, "Where's Corey ? Can he get y'all?"

"I don't know yet, I was in the middle of talking to him when you called." There was a second or two of silence and then I said, "I've been trying to find a way out of the city without getting on a plane. Everybody seems to be clueless as to what's going on. I tried to walk to the house, but was stopped and turned around by a military roadblock or whatever. I'm about to go and walk down to a checkpoint a few miles past the airport on Airline Highway toward Baton Rouge because someone told me they might let people through to pick up folks from the airport."

"Call me or text me when you find out."

"Hey Lora. Listen! Just in case my phone doesn't work ... keep in touch with me by text messaging and keep in touch with Corey. Get a pen and write his number down!"

Hurriedly she said, "Hold on a minute!" I looked at my phone and saw the charge was dwindling down quickly. "All right, what's his number?"

I gave her the number and said to text message Corey if she needed to. Then, I lost the call.

You've gotta be kidding me.

I tried to call her back about five times with no success. I didn't realize it, but I had walked about a hundred yards away from our area. I turned around and went back to tell everybody, "Hey y'all, I'll be back in a little while. I'm gonna walk down to the checkpoint on Airline toward Baton Rouge to see if they're letting cars through to pick people up!"

Someone asked impatiently, "How far down is it?"

"About three miles, I think."

Someone else said, "Do your thang, G!" I waved back without even looking and away I went.

I decided to turn my phone off for a little while to conserve the battery. With no way to charge it and the battery getting low, I figured that would be best. I was walking right in the direction of the setting sun and it was blazing hot. You would think by now I would have been used to heat, but it was wearing me down.

About half a mile from the airport is an overpass bridge that goes over some railroad tracks, and once I was over the other side, I could see the checkpoint way down the road. It looked like an eternity, like a mirage, but in reality it was a couple of miles down the road. I walked another half a mile or so and a couple of cars passed me by. I decided to see if I could hitchhike (this would be a first) down to the checkpoint to conserve some energy.

About two minutes later, two African-American guys in a truck passed me by, then they stopped, pulled over, and started to back up. I jogged about 50 yards or so to meet them. "Hey guys, can I catch a ride down to that checkpoint there? I'm trying to get some information from them!"

"Yeah, no problem. Hop in the back there."

"Thanks!" I jumped in the back and sat on a spare tire.

The breeze felt great. Simple things mean a lot when you're down to nothing. It was the first time I had cooled off in days, at least for a few minutes until we started to slow down near the checkpoint. As we came to a stop I stood up and jumped out, walking up to the front to thank them. One of the checkpoint guys pointed to us and said, "Wait a minute!" I stood there as this guy walked up to us.

"Is everything all right?"

"Yes, sir ... I was walking from the airport down to you to find out if we could be picked up by a friend or family member, and these guys were nice enough to give me a ride a couple of miles back." The cop, or whatever he was, told me to go talk to another guy across the street. I turned and thanked the guys for the ride again as I walked over across the street and looked over my shoulder back toward them, the checkpoint cop was asking the young black men for their driver's licenses or some sort of paperwork.

I hope I didn't get those guys in trouble.

The other officer across the street appeared to be a little more approachable. "Excuse me sir. Can I ask you a question?" While he was checking someone's driver's license, he said, "Yeah, go ahead."

"I heard back at the airport if we can get a friend or family member to come and pick us up they could get through the checkpoint here. Is that correct?" It took him a second to answer me as he was waving a car forward.

"That's correct, if the person can prove they're from this area or have a valid driver's license with proof of ownership of the vehicle being driven, we will let them through."

An indescribable feeling of relief came over me. "Thank you very much! See you later!" I turned around to walk back to the airport; the guys in the truck who had given me the ride were driving off past the roadblock. They must have passed whatever inspection was necessary to move on.

Prisoners of Katrina

I had renewed energy as I began my walk back to the airport. No matter if we had to sleep at the airport all weekend long, I now knew we did not have to get on a plane. Figuring this would be a good time to turn my phone back on, I did just that. I tried to call Lora a couple of times with no success. I then text messaged her saying, "THEY WILL LET U COME THROUGH CHECKPOINT TO GET US. CALL OR TEXT ME. GAV" After the "messaged sent" signal flashed, I tried to call Corey a few times with no success. I frantically text-messaged him saying, "COREY TRY AND CALL ME BACK. THEY WILL LET U THROUGH THE CHECKPOINT ON AIRLINE HWY. TEXT ME IF U CANT CALL ME. GAV."

I decided just to walk back. I didn't want anyone to give me a ride, just in case they didn't have the necessary documents for their cars, and then I would get arrested or something stupid like that. About five minutes later, my phone vibrated and the screen read, "DID U TALK 2 COREY? CAN HE PICK U UP? LORA"

Wiping the sweat from my brow, I sent back, "NOT YET. DID U TALK 2 HIM? I JUST SENT HIM A MESSAGE THAT HE COULD GET THROUGH CKPOINT."

I noticed I was walking faster than before, and by the time I sent the second message I had walked quite a bit closer to the airport. I was completely covered in sweat, as the sun continued beating down on my back and head. I looked and saw a truck turned over and a house with the roof half blown off. The area between the checkpoint and the airport was mainly filled with commercial businesses. It seemed like most of them sustained some sort of damage with blown out signs, torn off roofs, broken windows, and debris everywhere.

My phone rang and Lora's number flashed on the screen. "Hello! Hello? Can you hear me?"

"Bay ...bee ...?" Then "CALL LOST."

I tried to call back with no luck. I then tried Corey with no luck. I was starting to get desperate. How the hell can the phone work a couple of miles away under a concrete and metal down ramp with hundreds of people using their phones, but it won't work out here in the wide open with no other phone in use?

And at the worst time!

About 30 minutes later, I was nearing the airport, and there was a half-destroyed gas station on the right before the overpass bridge I had crossed before. About a 100 feet off, a woman pulled a suitcase behind her toward me. When I got closer I could see she was wearing green nursing scrubs. She waved to me to come over as she walked toward the door of the beat-up gas station. Once I got close to her, she said, "Is this place open?"

It was obvious to me it wasn't, but I didn't want to be rude. "No, I don't think so. Do you work at OPCSO (Orleans Parish Criminal Sheriff's Office)?"

"Why yes. Do you?"

"Yep, on HOD-10," I said, sticking my hand out and

introducing myself. She did as well, but I don't remember her name.

She said she worked at CCC, which is the building across from HOD. She then said, "You're not going to Baton Rouge, are you?"

Pointing behind me, I said, "No, I just walked down to a checkpoint a few miles down the road, and they said that if you can get someone to pick you up, they will let them through to the airport. Most of my family is in Texas, so I don't know when I'll get outta here, but I'm not getting in any of the lines or flying on any plane."

"Me neither, I'm gonna try and catch a ride to Baton Rouge, I guess."

Thinking about what Lora said, about the people stealing cars and ramming into other cars, I decided to warn her about what was going on the roads. She didn't seem too concerned. I looked around for a second or two and said, "Well, good luck. It was nice to meet you."

"You too."

As I got about a quarter mile away from the front exit of the airport, I could see a big jumbo cargo-looking plane take off in the distance. The closer I got to the front of the airport I saw people scattered everywhere. Groups of people sat in the grass, under trees, by the side of the road, and walking in every direction. There were thousands of people all over the place as I neared the entrance. I could hear the occasional person or group of people saying, "I ain't gettin' on no plane!"

"We gotta get on a plane; we got nowhere to go!"

"I'll walk outta this mutha' fucka' before I get on a plane!"

"Are you crazy — you stupid!?"

It was amazing to hear the different people arguing about what to do. It was like a mass mental breakdown.

Approaching my dad and the others, I noticed most of the civilians and workers from the HOD building were sitting or standing from the end of the down ramp all the way to our area under the down ramp and beyond. I wasn't sure if people knew it or not, so I told a few people if they could get a ride out of here, or get someone to pick t hem up, they could. I was immediately bombarded with questions.

"Where did ya hear that, G?"

"Are you sure? You gotta ride or somethin'?" and other questions like that.

It had been a few hours now, and there was still a lot of uncertainty as to what was going on. The sun was again starting to set exquisitely in the distance. Just about everybody with a cell phone was trying to make calls, borrowing each other's phones or trying to send text messages. I sat down next to my dad and tried to get comfortable on the concrete. Just as I leaned back, I felt something biting my lower right leg. Sitting up and slapping my leg, I saw a little bit of blood on my fingers. There were the remnants of a squashed mosquito. I said, "Great. With everything else going on we're gonna catch West Nile virus sitting here waiting to get outta here!"

My dad sat up and said, "What did you say?"

"Have you been getting bitten while I was gone?"

Looking a little confused he said, "Bitten by what?"

Trying not to look concerned I said, "I just killed a mosquito on my leg, and I hadn't noticed any before now."

"I don't think so, Son, but I don't know."

Over the past few years in Southwestern Louisiana and, for that matter, the Southern United States, there have been quite a few deaths from the West Nile virus. Most deaths have affected older people and, as you might imagine, if I was getting bitten by mosquitoes, my dad was probably getting bitten too.

The airport is located on the Jefferson Parish and Saint Charles Parish line and is surrounded by marshland to the west, with Lake Pontchartrain to the north. There are also low-lying areas around the airport that are perfect breeding grounds for mosquitoes.

Just as I was thinking of this, I saw my dad slap his right arm. He looked at his hand and had a tiny bit of blood and a smashed mosquito thrashing about. "I guess they *are* biting me."

"This is just great; we gotta get the hell out of here!"

In my mounting frustration, I stood up and walked around for a minute or two, slowly walking toward the center of the down-ramp and my cell phone miraculously rang.

It was Corey.

I didn't even give him a chance to say anything. "Dude, you gotta come get us ! Please!"

"Gav, I'm waitin' for my dad to come back with his truck."

"Hey man, I walked down to a checkpoint on Airline Highway between the airport and the I-310 exit (west of the city), and they said they would let people through to pick people up at the airport. Can you get us tonight?"

"I think so bra'. How bad is it?"

"Unbearable! Now the mosquitoes are starting to bite us! I don't wanna get West Nile out here. I definitely don't want my dad to catch it either — it could kill him."

"Hey, do I need to bring my gun or what? The news has been showin' some crazy shit."

"Corey! Bring whatever you want. I would suggest you bring your gun permit if you have one, and your driver's license."

I didn't realize it, but I must have started pacing, and as soon as I walked from underneath the down-ramp the call dropped.

"Corey! Corey!" Looking down at my phone it showed "CALL ENDED" and how long the call had lasted; not long enough.

These damn phones. I looked up and realized both times I lost the call I was not underneath the down ramp. I went back under the ramp and called Corey back. It took three tries, but I was finally able to get through.

"Corey? Can you hear me?"

"Hey, we got Lora on Darlene's (Corey's wife) phone. We're gonna try and come get ya'll."

"Hey, Corey, the entrance to the airport is blocked by police and the military. We're probably gonna have to walk out to the front and meet you somewhere."

"Where at?"

I thought about it for a second or two and then said, "There's a Denny's right across the street from the main exit, but the sign is halfway destroyed from the storm. What time do you have now?"

"About 7:30p.m .... Wait, hold on a second ... Darlene is talkin' to Lora."

As I waited for the relay message from Lora to Darlene to Corey and then to me, I walked over to my dad, smiled, and said enthusiastically, "I think we may get outta here tonight some time."

My dad looked up at me and said, "I don't feel like going anywhere, Son. I'm exhausted. Let's just stay right here tonight and go home tomorrow."

Almost dropping my phone I said, "What? Are you kidding? If Corey can come and get us tonight we're gettin' the hell outta here, that's for sure."

Before my dad could respond, Corey said, "I'm gonna get my gun and stuff together and come and get ya'll."

Pumping my fist in the air with excitement I said, "Man, I can't thank you enough. What did Lora say?"

"She was cryin' I think. She wants to come and git ya'll, but your family and hers won't let her leave. Too dangerous on the road or some shit like dat!"

"Yeah, I heard there's all kinds of wild stuff happening on the roads. Before I forget, take my dad's cell phone number down because my battery is gettin' low and his has a little more juice than mine."

"Hold on. Let me git a pen and paper."

As I waited, I couldn't help but smile a little, but the smile quickly left my face as I slapped my neck, killing another damn mosquito. I could see I was on my way to a blood transfusion at that rate. "All right, Gav, give me the number."

I did and asked, "When do you think you'll be leavin'?"

"Within an hour or so. Hey, we don't have no power, just so you know. My parents have an RV that's runnin' off a generator, but they're stayin' in it. Y'all will have to stay at my house."

"I don't care if I gotta sleep in the garage. After where we've been, it doesn't matter."

Laughing a bit, he said, "Okay bra'."

"Corey, listen. I'll keep both phones on so call me when you're getting close because we're gonna have to walk from the main building out to Airline Highway to meet you."

"Okay Gav, I'll see you soon — hopefully!"

"Great. Thanks. Bye."

After hanging up the phone, I sat back down next to my dad, saying, "Why in the hell would you want to stay here and get eaten up by mosquitoes? Lyin' on the concrete when we can go to somebody's house and you could lie on a couch and not risk getting the West Nile virus? In case you haven't noticed, we're a buffet for the mosquitoes right now!"

"I'm just tired; I don't feel like moving."

He was fading fast.

"Well, Dad, it's too late. Corey is supposed to be on his way to get us."

"Who?"

He didn't have a clue who I was talking about. "My friend Corey. Remember I used to work for his dad about five years ago? They live out in the country away from all this madness."

My phone rang, and it was Lora. I could hardly hear her, "Hey, is Corey coming to get you?"

"He's gonna try. I hope they'll let him through the road block."

"I love you Gavin! I miss you like crazy. You know that, right?"

Holding back tears I said, "I love you too! Stay by the phone and if Corey can get me tonight, I'll call you to let you know."

She said, "How's your dad?"

Walking away from him so he couldn't hear anything I said, "I don't know. Mentally, I'm not sure how he's coping. He keeps saying somethin' about going home. I've explained to him a thousand times his house may not be there."

"Don't be impatient with him! You know how you are."

"I'm tryin, but it's hard. What's even worse is the mosquitoes are startin' to eat us up, especially me. He says he doesn't feel them much, but I don't know how he doesn't feel them. He's sayin' he's too tired to move anywhere tonight, but I'll drag him kickin' and screamin' if I have too."

"Listen, baby, just talk to him calmly. Do you want me to talk to him?"

"Nah. Thanks, baby ... I got it. I hope to see you soon. If Corey can't get me tonight, I'm just gonna sleep here and try again tomorrow, but I'm not getting on any plane."

"If Corey can't get you, hopefully things in the next day or two will improve enough that I can come and get y'all."

"Honestly, baby, I think I might try to walk past the roadblock somewhere so Corey can get us. Either way, we gotta get away from the airport, because it's only gonna get worse. Well, sweetie, my battery is getting low. Hey, do you have my dad's cell number?"

"I don't think so — give it to me!"

I walked back over by my dad and I gave her his number. Sitting down next to him, I said, "Lora says hi ... if we get to Corey's house soon, she will work on picking us up soon!"

I could hear Lora say, "Oohh! That sounded good. Maybe he'll like that."

My dad turned to me and said, "Well, if Lora can do that, then I guess we better get to whoever's house we're going to."

With some hopefulness for my dad I said to Lora, "I'll talk to you later baby ... love you!"

"Love you too, Gavin, bye!"

After hanging up, I grabbed a water bottle out of my bag and chugged it down. Exhausted and restless at the same time, I got up and walked over to the mobile medical unit to have a look. It was dark by now and the sounds of helicopters, the roaring of generators, and people talking and moving around like ants filled the moment. The airport's electricity must have been running on generators because there were only a few main halogen lights shining through the blackness of the night. I decided to go to the second level and take one more look to see how bad it was. As I made my way up the stairs, I could hear the hustle and bustle of people shouting and ranting. When I got to the top level, there was still a mass of people everywhere. I didn't even bother going any farther. As I turned around, I saw a group of people coming up the stairs with all their bags and belongings. "Y'all goin' to get in those lines?"

A couple of them said, "Yeah, we ain't got no choice. We got nowhere to go."

Walking back down the stairs, I prayed we could get out of there that night. Not even five seconds after walking outside, I had mosquitoes all over me. I was waving my arms around, swatting bugs and looking like a crazy person. I grabbed my phone to see what time it was: 8:46 p.m. I saw two men in a fistfight as four or five law enforcement officials ran to break it up. There were people lying all over the ground trying to get settled for the night. It seemed as if some people were going to fly out as soon as possible, and others were resigned to stay where they were until most people were gone.

I could see my dad swatting his neck along with a few of the other people sitting near us. "Mosquitoes bad, huh, Dad? You still want to stay here tonight?"

"All right, Son, you made your point. Where are we going again?"

"Hopefully, my friend Corey, who lives about 20 miles or so from here, can get through the police checkpoint and pick us up. Hopefully."

"Yeah, *hopefully*. I've heard that before."

I had to bite my tongue once again. I was doing the best I could and he didn't seem to appreciate it. I still wasn't sure he really knew the magnitude of what was going on. We'd gone from one serious threat to another all week.

Time crept by. With every swat and scratch of the mosquitoes, I was convinced one of us would end up sick. We had made it this far, and now we had to deal with this threat. I was more worried about my dad than myself, so I grabbed one of my shirts and fanned him. This served as a three-fold purpose: it kept me moving, hopefully keeping the mosquitoes off and it did the same for him; and it also gave him a breeze to keep him cool. I could see he appreciated it, but he didn't say anything. He forced a grin occasionally while shifting around trying to get comfortable.

The majority of people on the first level were under the down-ramp area because the main source of light was under there. Some people had dogs on leashes lying next to them. I would also sometimes see a dog wandering around without a leash. I began to wonder if some people just abandoned their pets or were unable to bring them on the departing planes. I also wondered where my mom was and if she was all right. From time to time I grabbed my phone to make sure I didn't miss a call or text message because sometimes, before the storm, my phone wouldn't ring or I would get a voicemail from the day before.

About 10 minutes later, I got a text message paging me to a phone number I didn't recognize. It had a "708" area code. *Where the hell is that?*

I leaned over and told my dad, "I'll be right back, I've gotta make a phone call."

"Who are ya calling, Son?"

"I'm not sure, Dad. This number popped up on my phone, and I have no clue who it is. I don't recognize the number." I put down my shirt and walked behind where we were to a spot that was a little less noisy, but I made sure to stay under the down-ramp.

I dialed the number a couple times without it going through, of course. On the third try it started to ring, but the tone was very low. After about three rings, a female voice answered, but I didn't recognize the voice.

"Gavin...?"

"Hello ... who is it? I can barely hear you."

"Gavin, it's your mother!"

A little stunned to hear her voice I said, "Mom! Is that you Mom?"

"Yes! Yes ... can you hear me?"

"Barely! Where are you?"

"I'm in Chicago at your Aunt Leslie's house. Where are you?"

"Dad and I just got evacuated to the airport a few hours ago from downtown, from work."

She must have sensed the desperation in my voice, "Son, are you all right?"

"It's been unbearably crazy the last five days. I don't know where we're goin' to end up. There's a slim chance I could end up in Texas somewhere on a military base under Marshal Law for weeks. I don't know. Dad is out of his medicine and keeps asking me when we're going home. It's chaos everywhere!"

"Did you say a military base in Texas?"

"Possibly. I'm trying to get my friend Corey to come and get us, but I don't know if he will be able to get through the roadblock."

There were a few seconds of silence before she said, "Did you say a roadblock? You're breaking up ..."

"Yes! There are military and police all over the place."

"You said your father is with you? Is he all right?"

"We've been through one hell of an ordeal, but he seems all right — physically, but I'm not sure mentally. You know how he is."

With a motherly concern in her voice, she said, "I love you, Son. Hang in there. Your father needs you. Be strong! I'll pray for the both of you."

"Mom, I have to save the battery on my phone, but I'm glad to hear your voice. Oh, before I forget, how's Alex (my half-brother)? Is he all right? Have you spoken to him?"

With a slight crack in her voice she said, "Not yet, but knowing Doc (Alex's father), they probably evacuated. I haven't been able to get through to his cell phone, but I'll keep trying."

"Well, I'm glad you're all right, Mom, and I'll call you as soon as I end up wherever I end up."

"I love you Gavin and I'm gonna pray for you and your father's safety!"

"Me too. Love you. Bye."

After hanging up with my mom, I felt a huge sense of relief that she was all right, but wondered if Alex was too. My gut told me he was alive, but I just didn't know. I sat back down next to my half-asleep dad. I swatted his right arm below his elbow, killing another mosquito.

Please God, let us get out of here tonight, please! Please, don't let anything happen to my dad!

Putting my head between my legs, I strained to hold back tears. Composing myself, I grabbed the shirt on top of my bag and started to fan my dad again. It was nighttime now and once again, the stars covered the sky. The people scattered on the ground level of the airport were starting to settle in to their areas, resigned to the fact they were going to be there for the night, if not longer. Everybody had some piece of cardboard or paper and fanned himself or herself to try and cool off. Occasionally, vehicles drove by, but they were few and far between. I didn't know if that meant they were only letting a few cars past the checkpoint or if it took a long time for each car to pass through it. After gazing in the general area of the exit, my phone vibrated again. The message read, "IN LINE AT CHECKPOINT. LINE IS LONG. WILL CALL IF WE GET THRU. COREY." I looked at the time, and it was about 9:30.

I decided not to say anything to my dad, knowing he wouldn't have anything positive to say.

Feeling ever so close to getting to some sort of safety, I continued to fan my dad relentlessly. I only felt a few bites. I did my best to keep the mosquitoes off of my dad.

Looking around it looked like a war zone. Just about everybody was sitting or lying on the ground, half asleep or slumped over. Obviously, the past four or five days had taken their toll. I was one of the few people standing, and to be honest, I didn't know how.

It was creeping upon 10:30. The charge on my phone was waning, and I was fearful it would go dead before we got out of there. Checking my dad's phone, I saw that his was about half-charged, but it didn't seem to be working that well. My dad was dozing, periodically wiping and scratching his face and irregularly snoring. I was beginning to think Corey wouldn't be able to get through to rescue us.

Not a minute later, my phone rang. It was him. "Hey dude, the line is barely moving ... I'm gonna try to go down River Road and cut through that way."

"Yeah, okay. Whatever you can do. I'll be waitin' for your call."

"All right, bra'... later."

Prisoners of Katrina

"Later."

It was so close I could almost taste it.

Freedom and safety, that is.

Well, not really, but I was really feeling better. At least he was trying to get to us. I knew he would do whatever he could to make it happen. All I could do was fan the old man and keep my fingers crossed Corey would get here without getting arrested or something.

For the next 45 minutes, I tried to keep my dad cool and reflected on the past few days. It was amazing to think about how much had changed in such a short time. I really liked my job and where we lived, and now everything had changed. I didn't realize it, but I was sitting down next to my dad drinking a bottle of water, and I didn't even remember getting the water out of my bag.

Finally it came. The call!

It was almost 11:30 on Friday night, September 2. Five days after Katrina came ashore in New Orleans, eight days after it hit southern Florida: "Hey Gavin, we're in front of the Denny's. Get your ass up here as fast as you can, before I shoot one of these mother fuckers walkin' around my truck!"

"All right, all right! Give me about 10 minutes. We have to walk from the main area to the exit. We're comin' right now!"

"Hurry up!"

I didn't even say "bye" as I ended the call. "Dad, wake up. We're leavin'!"

Disoriented he said, "I'm too tired to go anywhere."

"What? Get your ass up now! Corey is waiting for us. Get up! Get up!"

"All right ... all right, Son. Hang on a minute."

As I pulled up the bag he was laying on, Nurse Donna saw me gathering my stuff together and said, "Where the hell are you going?"

"We're outta here baby! I gotta get him away from these mosquitoes. My friend just called and said he is front of the Denny's waitin' for us."

"Well, Gavin, take care and good luck."

Leaning over and giving her a hug I said, "You too! I'll see ya ... good luck to y'all too!"

Grabbing both bags and putting one on each shoulder, I said goodbye to those around me. As we began to walk toward the exit, I didn't realize how many people I would see between the down ramp and the exit, but I said goodbye what seemed like a hundred times. It was really strange, but I felt like a chapter in my life was ending, and I realized I probably wouldn't see many of those people ever again.

My dad was trying to walk as fast as he could, swerving back and forth, and stumbling a couple of times. As we passed the bottom of the down-ramp, it was so dark I could hardly see. I had to stop a couple times to wait for my dad to catch up and to rest my shoulders from the weight of the bags. "I'm walking as fast as I can, Son ... I can't see too good in the dark."

"I didn't say anything, Pops. Take your time."

Approaching the exit, I could see what looked like Corey's

truck parked across the highway on the edge of the Denny's parking lot. Everything felt like it was in slow motion as we neared the truck. Police or military personnel (it was so dark I couldn't tell) were directing traffic and telling people to get off the road. I waved one over to me and said, "That's my ride over there (pointing about 50 yards away)."

"All right, hurry up and get across the street!"

I hooked my dad's left arm with my right as I grabbed my phone, balancing both bags on each shoulder. I called Corey as we walked across the street. "Dad, it looks like we made it out of the city alive!"

"What's that? Oh, yeah, I guess so ... where are we going again?"

"To Corey's house. Don't worry about it ... it'll be better than the airport, I promise."

Corey must have seen us coming across the street because he got out of his truck. "Hey bra', y'all get in on my side ... throw your bags in the back." As I threw my bags in the back, Corey helped my dad get into the back cab of the truck. Corey's wife, Darlene, was sitting in the front passenger's seat looking a little paranoid.

I saw Corey's handgun sitting on the center console. "You brought some firepower with you, I see."

Closing the door he said, "Dude, I was sure I was goin' to have to shoot somebody about five minutes ago. They had all kinds of sonsabitches walkin' around my truck!"

His wife said, "Yeah. It's so dark. We thought somebody was gonna try and carjack us!"

They both turned to my dad and said, "How ya doin?"

Not really sure who they were he said, "Oh, I don't know, okay, I guess."

I could see he was a little unsure, so I said, "Dad, you remember Corey. I used to work for his dad a few years ago, and this is his wife Darlene."

It took him a few seconds, but then he said, "Oh yeah, 'hi' Corey and what's your name again, Sweetheart?"

Smiling at me, she answered, "Darlene."

"Nice to meet you."

As he sat back, I said, "Hey y'all, thanks for comin' to get us — I can't thank you enough. If y'all wouldn't have come we might have been shipped out on a plane to Texas somewhere or a military base. That might have been worse than everything we've been through already."

Corey turned the truck around and we drove about a mile and then took a turn and drove toward River Road (a road on each side of the Mississippi River that snakes around for many miles in both directions). I eventually said, "Why are we going this way?"

Corey replied, "The line coming in was really bad so we cut through and down River Road, where some of those orange and white road blocks set up, but we went around 'em."

Sure enough, there was a "Road Closed" sign blocking the road up ahead and we went right around it. We eventually got to the I-310 loop that went south towards Highway 90 (south of the city). As we took the loop, there were no streetlights anywhere.

It was like we were driving through outer space, with only our headlights to guide us.

We made small talk with them for the next 15 minutes or so with my dad falling half asleep while we drove.

When we turned onto Bayou Gauche Road, Corey said, "Now, remember, we ain't got power at our house. My parents are staying in their RV, which is running off of a generator, and we'll be staying with them. During the day y'all can hang out in there."

Making sure he knew how grateful I was, I said, "Hey man, don't even worry about that. We'll be fine. I'm just lookin' forward to taking a shower. I haven't had one in about six days!"

Laughing, Corey said, "Yeah, I can tell!"

I laughed and Darlene slapped Corey on the shoulder, "Oh, Corey!"

After another second or two of laughter, I blurted out, "That's all right, Darlene. He's right!"

"Hey bra', you know it'll be a cold shower!"

"Man, I don't care if ice cubes come out of the shower head; I'm takin' a shower."

As we turned down his street, he asked us if we wanted something to eat. I kindly declined for my dad. I woke him up and told him, "We're here — let's go take a shower."

Corey grabbed his flashlight and led us inside. He and Darlene got us set up with pillows as I made a bed on the floor and made a bed on the couch for my dad. They had some water in an ice cooler and some snacks on the table for us. We thanked them again and they left and went down the street to his parents' RV. We navigated to the bathroom by flashlight, and I got Dad in the shower as I held the light over the shower curtain so he could see what he was doing. After he was done, I jumped in and let the frigid water run over my head and body.

"Wow," I said out loud.

"Boy, you said it!" my dad chimed in.

"This sure beats sleeping outside on the concrete while getting eaten up by mosquitoes!"

"You're right, Son!"

Corey had left us some clean T-shirts and shorts to sleep in, since all of our stuff was dirty and smelly. As we lay down to sleep, there were a few minutes of silence. As I was falling asleep, my dad whispered, "I love you, Son... thanks for getting us out of the city."

I reached up from the floor and patted him on the back, holding back tears and said, "Love you too, Buddy. You know I'll always be here for you. Goodnight."

"Goodnight, Son."

Within a couple of minutes, he was gently snoring and I drifted off too.

We'd made it.

Epilogue

THE NEXT MORNING WHEN I WOKE UP, it took me a moment or two to remember where I was. My dad was still asleep, or so I thought. I didn't hear him snoring, and I didn't hesitate to check to see if he was breathing. On cue, he let out a big snore as I was about to wake him up. Laughing to myself, I decided to let him sleep. I got up and went out the back door to check out the surrounding and to reflect on the past week.

What a week it was!

I took another cold shower, and my dad woke up about 9:30 or so, and like me, he didn't quite know where he was. Corey and Darlene came down from his parents' place and offered us some coffee and a hot breakfast. A smile came across my dad's face like I hadn't seen in quite a while. "Hell yeah!" he said, while he scrambled for his clothes and shoes.

For the rest of the day Corey's parents were out and about, and they let my dad and me stay in their motor home, where we had our first taste of real air-conditioning in over a week.

It was glorious.

They also had a television, and we were able to catch up on what was going on and how the country was reacting to this national disaster.

Since there was no electricity and the generators ran off of gas, they periodically turned off the generators to conserve energy. I noticed Corey's mom, Ms. Maxine, had some clothes hanging on a clothes line, and I asked her if I could wash our clothes since ours were all dirty. Smirking slightly, she directed me to a plastic tub, liquid detergent, and a water hose and said, "Here's the washing machine!" It was then that I got a glimpse of the old days, when the washing was done by hand and hung to dry. In order to get our clothes cleaner, I used the back of a shovel handle to churn the water and clothes. I was amazed to see the water turn a dark shade of gray. Who would have known in this day and age, clothes could get clean in by using a bucket?

It didn't take long for my dad to start asking, "When are we going home? I need to get my medication." I had to continue to explain to him what had really happened and there was no guarantee we had a home to go home to. I was able to call Lora. She said she and my two cousins, Scott and Craig (from Paris and McKinney, Texas), were coming to get us on Monday afternoon — hopefully.

"They're in the process of getting gas cans and filling them up so we can leave early Monday morning ... you need to decide where we can get y'all. José (my sister-in-law's boyfriend) said he can get y'all from Corey's and bring y'all somewhere off I-10 to meet us."

Just when I thought I would have some down time, I was right back on the phone talking with my wife, José, and others trying to get us to Texas. I had charged my phone on Corey's parents' generator and was able to use it without worry it would die.

My Aunt Sandra lives in Paris and told Lora she had a place for us to stay and a little cottage for my dad to stay in while we got our plans together. At least we had a place to stay, but I was faced with the proposition of telling my dad we were on our way to Paris, Texas, to stay for a while and not home where he desperately wanted to be.

After finally getting off of the phone, we sat around most of that evening as I told them what the city looked like after the storm blew through and about our adventures in the aftermath. After a nice home-cooked dinner, our first in a week, we were down the street getting ready to sleep. Although it was quite hot, it was nothing compared to the stench-filled sweltering heat we were in for six days.

Most of Sunday was spent finalizing our plans to get to Texas. I decided to check on my condo after hearing on the news Jefferson Parish was opening up (under curfew) for residents who wanted to assess their property damage. After speaking to José, I made a decision to catch a ride with him on Monday morning to Kenner to see how bad it was.

Our entertainment for the day came courtesy of my dad. We were sitting by the Katrina-polluted pool in the backyard of Corey's parents' house. It was steamy hot, so we moved under the back patio into the shade. In south Louisiana, there are countless numbers of critters, and we have millions of "love bugs" (they mate for 24 hours and die) during the late summer. As we sat around and shot the breeze, my dad started swatting love bugs away from him. This was funny by itself.   About five minutes later, he looked to his left and saw the wooden gate open. We watched him get up, mumble something, and walk over to the gate and close it. As he sat back down he announced to us, "Maybe if we keep the gate closed, we can keep those damn bugs out!" We all looked at each other, smiling and trying to hold back our laughter. He was serious, too. I realized he was so exhausted he had mentally slipped a little more. I hadn't been able to see him as much in recent years, but after spending that week with him up close, I concluded we were at the point in our lives I had been dreading for a long time.

You can't escape Father Time, and as much as my dad likes to think he's 50 years old, he's not. From then on, I would be keeping a close eye on him.

On Monday morning, I was on the phone again. Lora called and said they were on their way from Texas, and we decided to meet in LaPlace (a suburb further west from the airport) in the early afternoon. We agreed to stay in contact with each other periodically throughout the day. I then made arrangements with José to go into Kenner to see how bad the condo was. Corey's wife gave me a ride to Corey's work, and he gave me a ride to LaPlace because he didn't want her to drive without him. I couldn't really blame him.

That turned out to be a mistake!

José and I agreed to meet in the Home Depot parking lot in LaPlace and then take Airline Highway into Kenner. This is about a 12- to 14-mile stretch of road and was the only main road into town, as the I -10 at LaPlace was closed to incoming traffic. Once we got to Home Depot and met José and his friend, reality struck.

There was a line of cars, in both lanes, bumper-to-bumper for as far as I could see leading into the city and back to the west toward Baton Rouge. I understood I would be unable to get into Kenner, assess the damage, and get back in time to meet Lora and my cousins. Also, it would take extra time for them to get into LaPlace. We made a decision to go back to Bayou Gauche and then to Raceland via Highway 90. As we made our way back, we had to go down River Road toward Baton Rouge, over the Sunshine Bridge and back to Bayou Gauche to pick up my dad. The next time I was able to speak to Lora, they were just passing through Baton Rouge, making great time. Unfortunately, I had to tell them to turn around and come back through Lafayette, going south through Houma down Highway 90 so we could meet them in Raceland somewhere.

We made the decision to meet at the Shell station on Highway 90 in Raceland. After we packed me, my dad, José's friend, his dog, and José into his Nissan Altima, I thanked Corey and his family for everything they had done for us. We said our goodbyes and then we made our way to the gas station, which was about 15 miles from Corey's house.

Once we were dropped off at the Raceland Shell station, my dad and I sat in the mini-restaurant area. Before long, he was up and roaming around the store as I struck up a conversation with a guy who was sitting down to eat. Come to find out the man owned some businesses about a half-mile from my home, and he described the scene to me. I'll spare you the details, but from what he said, his places had substantial damage, and I could only assume mine did as well.

It was after 3 p.m., and my dad had purchased some clip-on sunglasses and a bunch of junk food. As he stuffed his face, I got a call from my cousin Scott, who said, "Is there anyway you can hitch-hike from where you are down the road a few miles or so? We're at some sort of checkpoint and there are a bunch of cars in front of us. It could take hours from here to get to y'all. I'll pay big money to anyone in there who'll give you guys a ride." I told him I'd call him back in a couple of minutes as I stood up to start looking around to see who I could ask for a ride.

The man I was talking to eventually agreed to give us a ride, but I had to convince him first, because it was in the opposite direction of town. He kept insisting that he just came through a roadblock and was sure I was telling him the wrong way. Once I was able to convey to him we were going the other way, he finally realized he was turned around and said, "You're right — let's go!" I rounded up my dad, grabbed our stuff, and we got in this man's truck. I called Scott, told him we had a ride, that we were in a black truck and the guy who was bringing us would not go past the checkpoint. "That's great, Gavin. We'll cut across the median and back up to y'all!"

As we approached the checkpoint, our side of the road was clear, with no one stopping and no one checking any cars. The other side had a few police units and, I guess, state policeman checking every car. Both lanes were full of cars as far as I could see, and I had no idea how far down Lora and my cousins were. The man who drove us said, "This is as far as I'm gonna go fellas." I called Scott back and told him to cut across the highway and we were on the side of the road in a new black Ford truck. Not even 10 seconds later, I could see a white Chevy Suburban about a mile down the road sharply cut across the grassy median and backing up down the shoulder toward us.

As we got out of the truck, I thanked the man for the ride, grabbed our bags, and put one on each shoulder. It didn't take them long to get to us and as they stopped and got out, I immediately made eye contact with Lora and we both let out a sigh of relief. I couldn't believe how thin her face looked; in just nine days she had lost a good deal of weight. I knew she was worrying, but I could clearly see how this ordeal took its toll on her. I shook hands and hugged both of my cousins and then hugged my wife as tightly as I could, both of us wordlessly shedding a few tears.

I could hear Scott thanking and offering the man who had given us a lift some money, but the man said, "No thanks, that's all right." Out of the corner of my eye , I saw my dad walking toward Scott and Craig, shaking their hands and letting out a sigh of relief.

We eventually put our bags in the back of Scott's Suburban and drove off toward the setting sun.

This part of the journey finally ended in Paris, Texas at about midnight. After 10 hours, we finally got to the room at the Best Western where Lora and her family had been staying.

Finally! Whew!

A few days later, I rented a car and drove back to New Orleans to see how bad the damage was to my home. The drive was dreamlike. I still couldn't believe everything that had happened. With all the gas shortage concerns, I stopped about seven or eight times before I got to the city limits. It was during this drive I made the decision to write a book.

For some reason, I felt I was supposed to be in it, and it was meant to be. Hopefully, things would work out. I first went to my dad's house to see how it fared. To my surprise, his place had minimal damage, and I was able to save his treasured instruments: a saxophone, clarinet, and a flute. After spending about three or four hours cleaning out his refrigerator and throwing out some stuff that got wet from a couple of leaks, I left and made the long drive to our house to assess the damage.

After navigating through the numerous military checkpoints, I arrived at our home. The damage was pretty bad. About three feet of water was pooled in the downstairs portion of the condo and a six- to eight-foot area of the ceiling in the master bedroom had caved in. I vividly remember looking around in shock, not knowing where to begin the clean-up process.

Navigating around all of our water-logged stuff, the smell was horrid. I could only assume with all of the flooding, some of the nasty-looking water from a nearby canal made its way into our house. The smell could have also been from the water just sitting in our house for a while; I really don't know. The back patio area looked like a bomb had gone off. The fence was gone and most of the plants and vine trellis was destroyed. I really believe that a twister or something must have caused the ceiling in the bedroom to cave in and destroy the backyard. Mine is a corner unit and the building right behind had much less damage. I attempted to clean up the place for a few hours and punched holes in the sheetrock, (as advised by a neighbor), so the mold wouldn't spread as fast.

As the evening approached, I left and spent the night at Corey's house. I brought some of our salvageable pictures to his house. The video tape of my wedding was in the downstairs T.V. stand and had been completely submerged in water and still very wet. Corey suggested putting it in the refrigerator to get the condensation out, and to my surprise we later played the video and found it worked.

The next day I went back to my dad's place to finish cleaning up, which was another six or seven hours of hot, hard work. Once I was finished with that, I drove back down the West Bank Expressway, taking a mental note of all the wind damage to countless businesses and homes. It was hard to look at so much devastation, but after what my father and I went through, it really didn't surprise me. I eventually made it back to my house, did some more cleaning, and drove back to Texas to be with Lora and the dogs.

The time away gave me a chance to get closer to my family. Being the youngest cousin on my father's side by quite a few years, I really never had the chance to be close to my cousins and my Aunt Sandra. My Aunt Sandra was married to my dad's brother, my Uncle Tommy, who died about 15 years ago. Although I didn't know it, his death really affected my dad quite a bit. During the time before and after I arrived in Texas, Scott and his mother were wonderful to Lora and her family. As a matter of fact, the whole city of Paris, Texas, was wonderful to them, along with all the other Louisiana evacuees who ended up there.

We stayed in Texas for almost a month. Lora eventually got a call to go back to work teaching at the school she was at before. On a whim, I called my supervisor at work and asked what was going to happen with my job. To my utter surprise, he said they were going to reopen the HOD building in mid-October. I asked him if they were going to bring anybody back and he said he would find out. A couple days later he called and asked if I could like to come back, and I jumped at the offer. There were over 70 nurses who worked at the jail before the storm and they only brought back 10 of us at first, which made me feel pretty good (and lucky). Besides, Lora and I really needed the health insurance to take our last try at the in vitro process. I went back to work in mid-October and was able to see the mass destruction first hand. We eventually found out the eggs were moved soon after The Storm and we pray they will be alright so we can try one more time.

Prisoners of Katrina

Of the numerous facilities within the jail system, only the HOD building, where my father and I were stranded, was salvageable to the point of re-opening the jail system for the city of New Orleans.

I really had to see it to believe it. The first building I went into was the CCC building. There were breaches in many of the tier walls. Those walls were made with cinder blocks and obviously were not made very well. I was told by one of the deputies fire extinguishers were used by the inmates to knock holes in the walls in an attempt to escape the facility. Some did escape, including a man from St. Bernard parish who was in for murder. He got as far as Mississippi before he killed another man and was caught.

In all, I have heard estimates there was over $100 million dollars in damage to the entire parish penal system, and from what I saw, that could be fairly accurate. All the buildings sustained heavy flooding, and many of them were beyond repair. I don't know what the future will hold for the city of New Orleans, but I will be able to watch firsthand what the new New Orleans will begin to look like. With everything that happened, I am still blessed my father was alive and we'd survived the ordeal of our lives together.

I was not able to find out what happened to the lady who was holding up the sign. I can only hope that she made it out. My little brother Alex made it out and would eventually go back to Waveland, Mississippi, to find where he lived was totally devastated. He stayed there for a while and eventually joined the Army and is currently in Iraq defending our country. He recently dodged death as he was in a

Humvee hit by a roadside bomb. Sustaining second degree burns and an injured knee, he was able to cut loose a fellow trooper and get them to safety under enemy fire. God bless him.

I have been working at the facility ever since we came back to the city and have not seen J.W. since. I hope he is all right and getting the psychiatric treatment he so desperately needs.

Nurses Robert, Donna, Urban, Favis and a few others have come and gone since. As we were evacuating, there were many times when I didn't think I would see those people again. I am glad I did and have formed a closer bond with them because of what we went through.

The only person I heard about that had a major physical problem was Deputy Lee. I found out about three months later Deputy Lee ended up in Houston and had three surgeries on that toe to try and save it. Unfortunately, the surgeries were unsuccessful, and he ended up getting the toe and part of his foot amputated.

As I move forward in my life, I will always remember this experience and keep it near to my heart. I know I will share it with generations to come. While I didn't appreciate the circumstances while they were unfolding, the experience shaped who I am and the choices I will make for the rest of my life.

THE END

The back side of O.P.P. which is connected to the New Orleans District Courthouse on the corner of Tulane Avenue and Broad Street in New Orleans.

The center building is House of Detention as seen from the Broad St. bridge. The CCC building is to the left.

Nurse Robert Gates who has been with
the Sheriff's office for over 15 years, mostly
working at the House of Detention.

Nurse Favis, LPN, who worked at the
Sheriff's office less than two years
when Hurricane Katrina hit.

John and Nurse Donna Landry

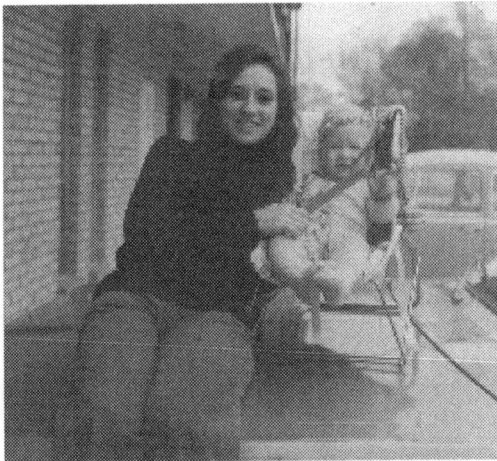

My mother, Roberta, with me, Gavin Johnson,
as a baby.

Lora and Gavin Johnson.

Dr. Marcus Dileo, whose heroic efforts saved many lives at Orleans Parish Prison in the aftermath of Katrina. He swam in contaminated waters to attend to others, with no regard for his own safety.

Liston Johnson, (playing clarinet) with his quintet in the good old days.

Liston Johnson, in the Gus Arnheim Band (immediate right of Gus), Los Angeles, 1942.

My father (third from left, front row) in a school band in his youth.

My father (far left on clarinet) in Ina Hutton Band, 1946. Al Hirt is in the back, top row.

My father, Liston Johnson in Army
uniform during World War II.

My friend Corey Dufrene with his wife Darlene. They
drove in with a handgun for protection and rescued me
and my father from the New Orleans airport . They took
us to safety at his parents' house in Bayou Gauche.

Gavin S. Johnson

Photograph by Roberta Wilson

The author, Gavin S. Johnson, a native New Orleanian, is a psychiatric nurse who worked at Orleans Parish Prison's House of Detention when Hurricane Katrina hit. A humble hero, he rode out the storm and its aftermath at the jail facility with his 83-year-old father, Liston, before getting them both to safety. This is his first book, a riveting and poignant story of survival and a son's undying love.

Prisoners of Katrina

Gavin S. Johnson

www.ingramcontent.com/pod-product-compliance
Lightning Source LLC
Chambersburg PA
CBHW031152270326
41931CB00006B/238